United States
Department of
Agriculture

Forest Service

Southern
Research Station

General Technical
Report SRS–143

Appalachian National Scenic Trail Pilot Survey

Stanley J. Zarnoch, J.M. Bowker, H. Ken Cordell,
Matt Owens, Gary T. Green, and Allison Ginn

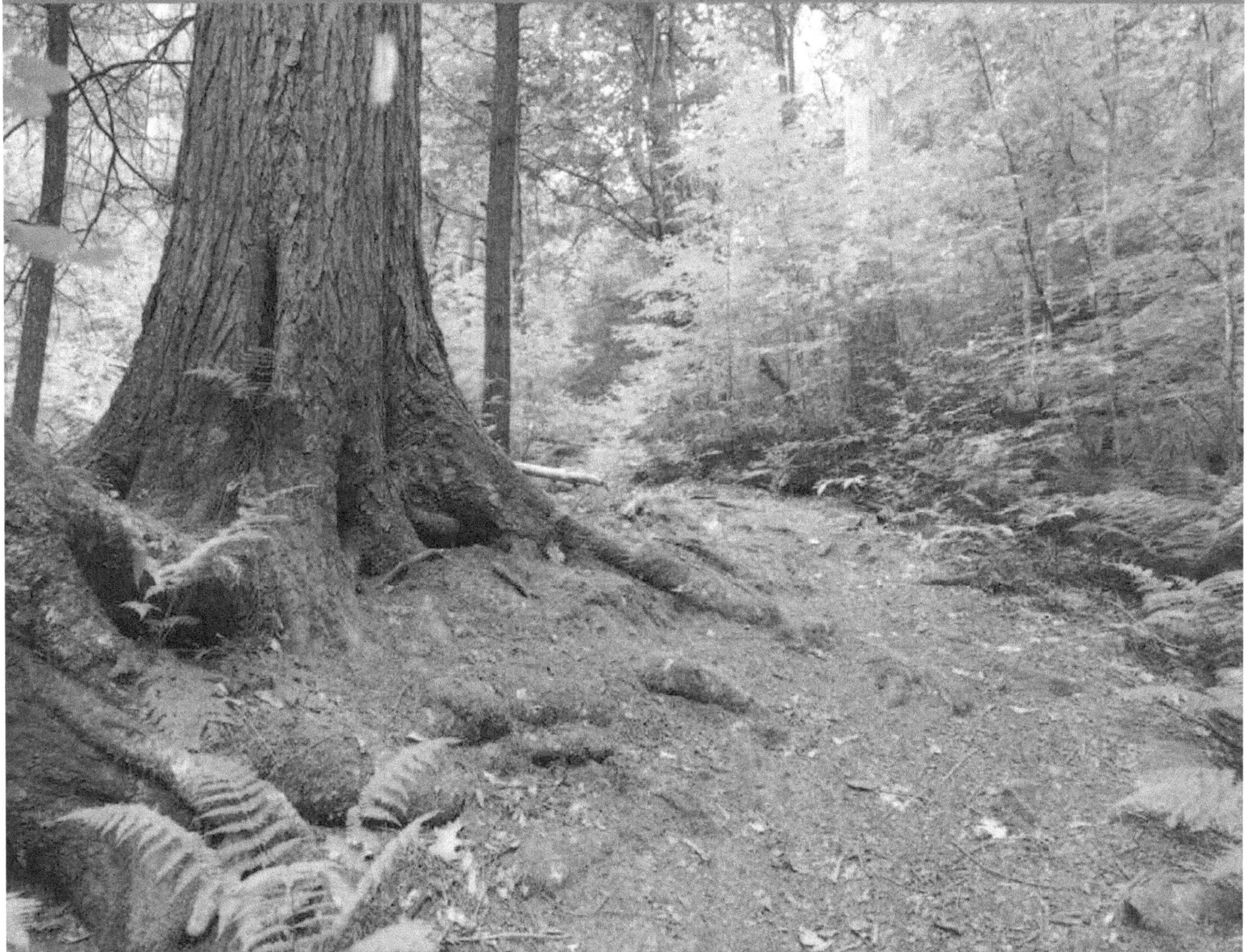

Authors:

Stanley J. Zarnoch, Mathematical Statistician, U.S. Forest Service, Southern Research Station, Asheville, NC 28804; **J.M. Bowker**, Research Social Scientist, and **H. Ken Cordell,** Pioneering Research Scientist, U.S. Forest Service, Southern Research Station, Forestry Sciences Laboratory, Athens, GA 30602–2044; **Matt Owens,** Research Professional, **Gary T. Green**, Assistant Professor, and **Allison Ginn**, Graduate Assistant, University of Georgia, Athens, GA 30602–2044.

September 2011

Southern Research Station
200 W.T. Weaver Blvd.
Asheville, NC 28804

Appalachian National Scenic Trail Pilot Survey

Stanley J. Zarnoch, J.M. Bowker, H. Ken Cordell,
Matt Owens, Gary T. Green, and Allison Ginn

Acknowledgments

This report was prepared for the U.S. Department of the Interior, National Park Service in partial fulfillment of Interagency Acquisition Agreement R2490050022 between the National Park Service, the Appalachian National Scenic Trail, and the U.S. Forest Service, Southern Research Station.

We are very grateful to many people for donating their time and effort to support this project. Volunteers assisting with pilot study field interviews were Joe Brookreson, Susan Brookreson, Donna Brother, Bob Cave, Polly Cave, Jessica Compton, Bob Fletcher, Jeannine Gaylor, Fran Huesman, Tom Johnson, Gale Kooser, John Roth, Dick Martin, Thyra Sperry, Kristi McKinley, Doris Morgan, Jean Neeley, Wendy Pacek, Dick Potteiger, Annie Powell, Barb Powell, Chelsea Powell, Ryan Sharp, Julie Strack, John Tatara, Barbara Van Horn, and Celeste Wiser. Also, thanks to Dave Winter of Leave No Trace Center for Outdoor Ethics for educational materials.

A number of local and regional Appalachian National Scenic Trail club members were instrumental in assisting with exit volume classifications for site days outside the pilot study region. These included: Laura Belleville, Scott Birchman, Dave Boone, Bill Boudman, Adam Brown, Julie Clemmons, Walt Daniels, Dave Field, Chris Firme, Jim Foster, Robert Freeman, Eleanor Grasselli, Dave Hardy, John Hedrick, Casey Horrigan, Tom Johnson, Mariah Keagy, Jim Lowe, Anne Maio, Howard McDonald, Gary Monk, Gail Neffinger, Andrew Norkin, Edward Oliver, Dan O'Neal, Dave Patrick, Jim Pelletier, George Ritter, Ron Rosen, Sara Sheehy, Julio Stephens, and Kerry Wood.

In addition, there were three trail clubs in the pilot survey area that warrant special recognition for their assistance throughout the course of this project. These include the Potomac Appalachian Trail Club, the Mountain Club of Maryland, and the Cumberland Valley Appalachian Trail Club.

The Appalachian Trail Conservancy provided much needed assistance with logistics, contracting, and interviewing. Interviewers included Howard Crise, Dave Heath, and Sara Woll. Administrative personnel including Karen Lutz, Steve Paradis, Laurie Potteiger, Matt Robinson, and Bob Sickley merit special mention.

Many Federal agency personnel also donated substantial time and effort to this project. National Park Service employees providing considerable assistance included Rita Hennessey, Don Owen, Todd Remaley, Butch Street, and Pam Underhill. U.S. Forest Service employees providing much needed assistance included Don English, Marilyn Howard, Pete Irvin, Sue Kocis, and Shela Mou.

We thank numerous people who provided constructive reviews of an earlier draft, which includes J. David Reus, Steve Paradis, and Bob Sickley of the Appalachian Trail Conservancy; Lynne Seymour and Ashley Askew of the University of Georgia; Chris Siderelis of North Carolina State University; and Ray Souter of the U.S. Forest Service.

Finally, very special thanks is due Bob Gray (retired), formerly the National Park Service's Chief Ranger on the Appalachian National Scenic Trail, for recognizing the need for such a study, obtaining the financial and political support, and ensuring that the study got off the ground.

Contents

List of Tables

List of Figures

Appalachian National Scenic Trail Pilot Survey

Stanley J. Zarnoch, J.M. Bowker, H. Ken Cordell,
Matt Owens, Gary T. Green, and Allison Ginn

Abstract

Visitation statistics on the Appalachian National Scenic Trail (AT) are important for management and Federal Government reporting purposes. However, no survey methodology has been developed to obtain accurate trailwide estimates over linear trails that traverse many hundreds of back-country miles. This research develops a stratified random survey design which utilizes two survey instruments, exit-site tallies and a survey questionnaire, to obtain visitation estimates on a portion of the AT. The design identifies three components (standard site days, augmented site days, and special events) which can be used to subdivide the sampling frame into estimator types that lead to more efficient sampling and estimation processes. In addition, design-based and model-based approaches are used to obtain estimates for comparison purposes.

The survey was performed from June 1 through August 14, 2007, on a 109-mile stretch of the AT from Harpers Ferry, WV, to 10 trail miles north of Boiling Springs, PA, at the Scott Farm. Visitation estimates were 66,967 for the design-based approach and 70,912 for the model-based approach, with coefficients of variation of 23 and 16 percent, respectively. Individual strata-level visitation estimates were quite variable and differed substantially between the two approaches.

An extrapolation to the entire trail for the whole year was performed by developing an appropriate sampling frame from which the strata weights could be obtained. Using the model-based approach and assuming the survey data were representative, the 2007 annual visitation extrapolation for the entire trail was 1,948,701 with a coefficient of variation of 20 percent.

Keywords: Design-based estimator, Lincoln-Petersen estimator, mark-recapture estimator, model-based estimator, recreation trail use estimation.

Introduction

The Appalachian National Scenic Trail (AT) (see appendix A for a list of acronyms and abbreviations) is a continuous marked footpath extending more than 2,175 miles across the Appalachian Mountains from the summit of Mount Katahdin in Maine to the summit of Springer Mountain in Georgia (fig. 1). It forms a greenway that connects more than 75 public land areas in 14 States. The AT was conceived in 1921, completed in 1937, and established as the first National Scenic Trail by Congress with the passage of the National Trails System Act in 1968 (Appalachian Trail Conservancy 2009). Consisting of over 250,000 acres that were acquired by the National Park Service (NPS) and the U.S. Forest Service (USFS), it is a component of the National Trails System and a unit of the National Park System.

Information on AT visitor use is important to help agency managers and planners identify where resources and funds should be utilized. In addition, the data serves as a valuable component of the NPS Public Use Data Collecting and Reporting Program whose objectives are (1) to design a statistically valid, reliable, and uniform method of collecting and reporting public use data for each independent unit administered by the NPS; (2) to enact a variety of quality control checks to eliminate errors; (3) to provide analysis and verify measurements of the public use data; (4) to assure consistency of data collection within units of the NPS; and (5) to support the continuous collection and timely publication of public use data (National Park Service 2009b). Moreover, information is required so that each park unit can report annually on service-wide and park goals. For instance, the NPS Government Performance and Results Act goal examines visitor safety incidents in terms of 100,000 visitor days. However, lacking a visitation survey, the AT administrators cannot accurately report to this important national objective.

Despite the need for such AT visitation information, a statistically valid, reliable, and uniform method of collecting and reporting public use data for any of the national trails has never been developed. Individual park and forest units, along with researchers, have collected some data on AT hikers and back-country users, particularly about user characteristics, attitudes, and preferences (Kyle and others 2004, Manning and others 2000). In addition, use has been statistically estimated on some smaller trails which intersect the AT, like the Virginia Creeper Trail (Bowker and others 2004, 2007). However, there has never been a trailwide study of AT visitation. Several years ago the Appalachian Trail Conservancy (ATC) produced an estimate of 2 to 3 million annual visitors on the AT. More recently, the NPS (2009a) and the ATC (2009) report on their Web sites that estimated annual visits number between 3 and 4 million. Unfortunately, documentation on the estimation methodology is not available and visitation was not categorized into day use, overnight use, nonrecreational use, or related categories. The ATC Web site also reports that thru-hikers have increased steadily over the past 5 decades, but have declined annually in number from 625 to 500 between 2001 and 2007. While the information on thru-hikers is likely accurate, they comprise an important but very small portion of overall AT use.

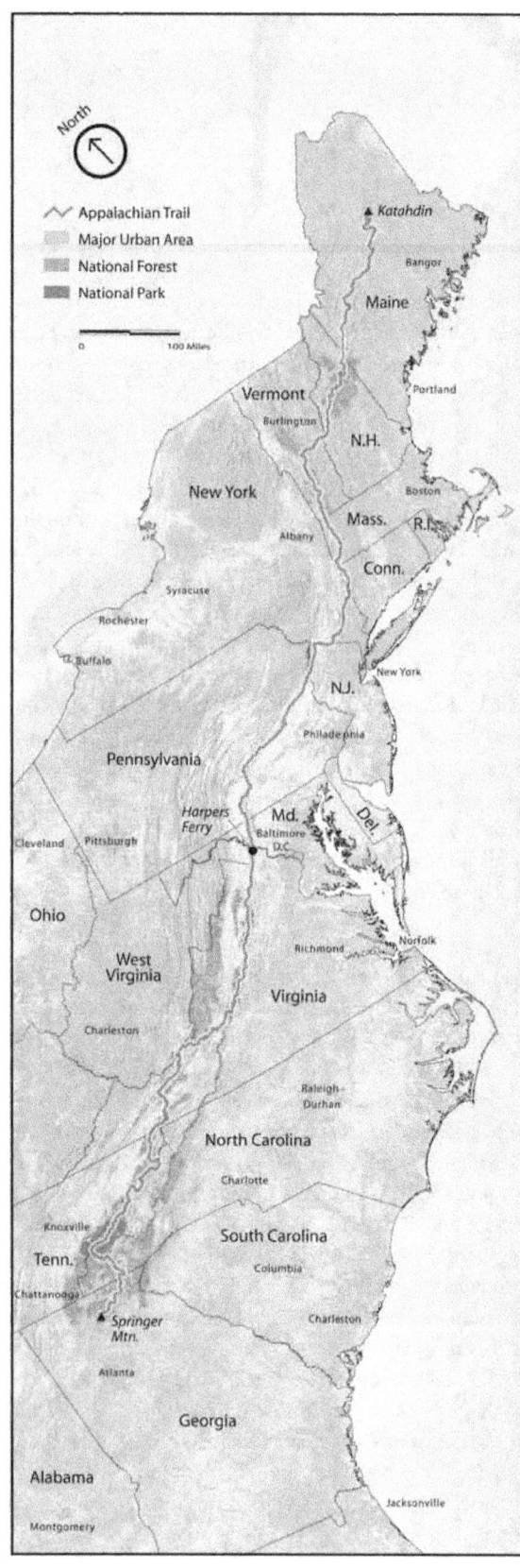

Figure 1—The Appalachian Trail is a 2,175-mile continuous trail across the Appalachian Mountains from the summit of Mount Katahdin in Maine to the summit of Springer Mountain in Georgia.

The main objective of this study was to develop a pilot survey design for estimating AT visitation that can be used as a prototype for future estimates of visitation on the entire AT. The survey design and estimates would also provide measures of precision such as standard errors and confidence interval estimates. In addition, this would provide the basis for a survey design applicable to some or all of the other components of the National Trails System. A secondary objective was to use data from the pilot survey to develop a trailwide extrapolation (TWE) estimate that would provide a visitation estimate for the entire AT. Because of limited resources, the pilot survey was designed to collect data during a limited time (June to August) and spatial (109 miles) segment of the AT. Thus, any extrapolation to the entire AT had to rely upon several assumptions. A final objective of the overall study was to design a survey based on information from the pilot survey which would include the approximate cost and effort required to conduct a statistically rigorous future survey of the entire AT. Sampling variability, logistical considerations, and operational constraints obtained in carrying out the pilot survey were to be incorporated into this future survey design.

Part I—The Pilot Survey

Overview

The objective of the pilot survey emphasized the methodological development of an efficient sampling strategy for estimating recreation visitation on a linear hiking trail. Although it was important to obtain a good estimate of visitation for the survey, this was not the most important issue. A small pilot survey is often used as a precursor to a larger, more complete and complex survey in order to gather experience and necessary information about the sampling problems that are encountered while designing and implementing the survey. Completion of a pilot survey typically exposes unforeseen technical, logistical, and methodological problems, thus, facilitating increased efficiency in a subsequent larger survey.

The pilot survey was applied to a 109-mile section of the AT extending from Harpers Ferry, WV, to 10 trail miles north of Boiling Springs, PA, at the Scott Farm from June 1 through August 14, 2007 (fig. 2). This section provided a complex yet representative snapshot of the AT because it traversed multiple States and natural resource areas, intersected other low-use and high-use outdoor recreation sites, and was within easy traveling distance of major metropolitan areas. In addition, it was convenient to offices of study cooperators (NPS, ATC) and had a history of strong local club affiliations that would be beneficial when recruiting volunteers to assist with the field survey. The time period for the survey was selected to coincide with a period of expected high AT visitation which would provide maximum survey data for analysis, expose any unforeseen

Pilot Study Area

N: Scott Farm, north of Boiling Springs, PA
S: US 340, south of Harpers Ferry NHP

Figure 2 — The pilot survey area from Harpers Ferry, WV, to 10 trail miles north of Boiling Springs, PA, at the Scott Farm.

survey problems that needed to be addressed in future surveys, and coincide best with recruiting volunteers to administer the field survey. Information obtained from the pilot survey was later used to satisfy other objectives which included completion of the TWE to the entire AT by using appropriate strata weights and a preliminary design of a total AT survey.

The approach for the pilot survey uses onsite sampling of exit sites to obtain average daily estimates of the number of last-exiting recreationists (LERs) which are then expanded to the total annual visitation estimate. The methodology is based upon the concept that if all exit sites are identified and the number of LERs is counted for each day of the survey period, the sum will be the total visitation for that time period. The pilot survey design was based in part on the USFS National Visitor Use Monitoring (NVUM) Program that has been developed to obtain visitation estimates for the national forests across the United States (English and others 2002, White and others 2007, Zarnoch and others 2002).

Some trail-use studies have incorporated a stratified random sampling design based on trail segments rather than exit sites wherein trail users were counted as they passed using either visual or electronic means (Lindsey and Lindsey 2004, Stynes 1996, Wolter and Lindsey 2001). However,

by counting LERs, we ensure that only recreationists will be included in the visitation estimate and that recreationists will not be "double counted" because they are exiting the site for the last time and, hence, will not return and exit to be counted again. An alternative approach that should give similar visitation estimates is to count only first-entering recreationists. However, other information such as length of stay, satisfaction with the facilities, etc., was also desired from the AT survey and obviously could not be obtained from first-entering recreationists.

The true visitation can only be obtained by counting all LERs from all exiting sites on all days throughout the survey period. This would be a complete census (Jacobi 2003) and, although it gives the correct visitation, a census would be cost prohibitive to administer over virtually all dispersed recreation areas and back-country trails, especially for a long trail like the AT. Thus, a sampling approach that would be more feasible was used to obtain an estimate of visitation along with the standard error and confidence intervals.

The AT pilot survey was based on a stratified random sampling design (Cochran 1977) subsequently adapted to trail, wildland, and other recreation-use estimation (Bergstrom and others 1996, Bowker and others 2004, English and others 2002, Gregoire and Buhyoff 1999,

James and Schreuder 1971). The sampling frame consisted of the population of all possible recreation site days—a collection of all days at exiting sites that were open for recreation along the pilot survey area. These site days were then placed in 15 potential strata consisting of 5 site-types and 3 use-levels. Within each stratum, a random sample of site days was selected which was visited by personnel who administered the onsite field survey. The main benefit of stratification was to reduce the standard error of the visitation estimate. Stratification also allowed a more controlled allocation of the sample throughout the population of site days and provided separate visitation estimates for each stratum which may be of interest for addressing various management issues.

Sampling Design

Sampling frame—The first step in the pilot survey, called prework, developed the sampling frame consisting of all site days along the AT from Harpers Ferry, WV, to 10 trail miles north of Boiling Springs, PA, at the Scott Farm from June 1 through August 14, 2007. A site day was defined as any day that a given site was available for LERs to be exiting. The formation of the population of site days required the identification of all exit sites along the pilot survey area of the AT; i.e., where a recreationist would possibly exit the AT, though not cross country. This was accomplished by using a combination of resources including Geographic Information System data, trail maps, and guide books as well as interaction with AT personnel and other people knowledgeable about the trail. Table 1 lists all 120 exit sites defined in the pilot survey area, giving their assigned site numbers, site names, and site-types (explained later). All sites were open for visitation during the pilot survey and, thus, each contributed 75 site days to the sampling frame implying a total of 9,000 site days.

The development of strata was based on site-type and use-level applied to each site day. The objective was to formulate strata such that all site days within a given stratum were as uniform as possible with regard to AT visitation. Generally, when this is accomplished successfully in a stratified random sampling design, the average visitation between all the strata will be as different as possible and the variation within each stratum will be as small as possible (Cochran 1977). This ideal situation is never met in practice, but if reasonably approximated, significant gains in precision of the visitation estimate are possible, resulting in smaller standard errors and narrower confidence intervals.

After reviewing the sites identified along both the pilot region and the whole AT, various patterns emerged that allowed the creation of several site-types. An exit site that simply consisted of a trail or road intersection across the AT was considered the trail/road (TR) site-type. If a parking lot was in the vicinity, as happened frequently where the AT intersected paved roads, then the site was a parking (P) site-type. It was presumed that both of these site-types would exhibit almost exclusive use by AT recreationists. In other areas there was a complex network of sites, some not clearly defined, with potential for considerable non-AT use. Examples of such included State parks through which the AT traveled for a considerable distance. These site-types were called multiple use (MU). There were also several AT sites identified that intersected Harpers Ferry, WV, a unique town and historical national park, which required the creation of a special site-type (HF). Here the overall AT and non-AT use were high and the intersection of the AT with the town was extremely complex (fig. 3) which did not resemble any of the other strata. The last site-type (ATCH) was unique to the pilot survey and consisted of the headquarters office of the ATC in Harpers Ferry, WV.

To further improve the stratification, the site days in each site-type were classified into one of three use-levels. These were low (L), medium (M), and high (H) depending on the anticipated number of LERs exiting from the site on the specific day. Note that this was based on the number of recreationists who were last exiting, not simply all exiting people, or people who were either passing through the site, or beginning an AT visit at the site. Also, these use-levels were specific to a given site-type. Thus, use-level L for site-type TR was different than use-level L for site-type MU. A simplified manner of referring to a given stratum is to combine the site-type and use-level. For instance, the stratum site-type TR and use-level L will be hereafter referred to as simply stratum TR–L.

Stratification was formed by the classification of all site days into the 15 potential strata formed by the combination of the 5 site-types and 3 use-levels. For the pilot survey, there were no site days in the TR–H or ATCH–L strata, thus, resulting in only 13 strata.

While performing the very time-consuming stratification of the site days with assistance from the ATC and local trail club staffs, it became evident that certain site days may have extremely high visitation due to special events in the vicinity. These site days were termed special events and were initially removed from the sampling frame. Here visitation was estimated in a different manner and added to the final visitation estimate. The only special event for the pilot survey was June 2, 2007, at Boiling Springs, PA, which was locally known as Foundry Day. The pilot survey sampling frame, thus, consisted of all site days for all the site-types (TR, P, MU, HF, and ATCH) from Harpers Ferry, WV, to 10 trail miles north of Boiling Springs, PA, at the Scott Farm during June 1 to August 14, 2007.

The well-known Mather Side Trail at Harpers Ferry, WV, was initially included in the sampling frame, but was later deleted for several reasons. First, it did not seem to fit into one of the five site-types previously defined. Although it most closely resembled site-type TR, it was felt that the proportion of LERs would be lower than the typical TR because it may contain a high proportion of non-AT

Table 1—The population of 120 sites in the pilot survey area from Harpers Ferry, WV, to 10 trail miles north of Boiling Springs, PA, at the Scott Farm

Site number	Site name	Site type	Site number	Site name	Site type
0	HF ATC HQ	ATCH	921	Locust Gap / Greenwd Furnace S	MU
809	US 340	TR	922	Locust Gap / Greenwd Furnace N	MU
810	(HF) VC shuttle parking	HF	923	Hosack Run Trail	TR
811	(HF) Shenandoah Street (20)[a]	HF	924	Ridge Road	TR
813	(HF) Lower Town	HF	925	Stillhouse / Ridge Road Sandy Sod	TR
814	C & O Canal Towpath E	TR	926	Road, Methodist Hill	TR
816	Keep Tryst (12)	P	927	Middle Ridge Road	TR
817	Keep Tryst Road	TR	928	Hill Road	TR
819	Weverton Road (30)	P	929	Dughill Trail	TR
825	Gathland State Park S (60)	MU	930	Ridge Road / Means Hollow	TR
827	Gapland Road	MU	931	Milesburn Road	TR
828	Gathland State Park N (35)	MU	932	Ridge Road	TR
829	Lambs Knoll Road N	TR	933	Rocky Knob trail	TR
832	Fox Gap (10)	P	934	Fegley Road	TR
833	Reno Monument Road	TR	935	Trail, unknown	TR
834	Dahlgren Campground	P	937	Big Flat (12)	P
835	South Mountain Inn (40) (US40A)	P	938	Dead Woman's Hollow (3)	P
836	Dahlgren Chapel (15)	P	942	Tumbling Run Game Preserve Road	TR
838	Monument Road	TR	946	Woodrow Road	TR
839	Washington Monument Road	MU	948	Michaux Road W	TR
840	Washington Monument Road S (10)	MU	949	Michaux Road E	P
841	Washington Monument Road N (40)	MU	950	Old Shippensburg Road	P
842	Washington Monument Road	MU	951	PA 233 (3)	P
844	Boonsboro Mountain Road (3)	P	953	(PGF) Bendersville Road W	MU
846	Boonsboro Mountain Road	TR	954	Store / Hostel / Intersection S	MU
848	Trail	TR	955	(PGF) Overnight / Dressing lot	MU
849	US 40 Annapolis Rock (50)	P	957	(PGF) Old Railroad Bed Road (8)	MU
853	Thurston Griggs side trail	TR	958	Pole Steeple trail	TR
857	Blackrock Road	TR	959	Old Forge Road	TR
864	Wolfsville Road / MD 17 W (5)	P	961	Trail, unknown	TR
865	Wolfsville Road / MD 17 E (10)	P	962	Limekiln Road	TR
867	Trail	TR	963	Tagg Run	TR
869	MD 77	TR	965	Pine Grove Road / Tagg Run (2)	P
872	Warner Gap Road (1)	P	967	Hunters Run /PA 34 (10) Zeigler	P
874	MD 491 / Raven Rock Rd.	TR	970	Road / Trash Can Alley (10)	P
875	High Rock (22)	P	973	PA 94	TR
878	Pen-Mar Road (40)	MU	975	Old Sheet Iron Roof Road (6)	P
881	Pen Mar High Rock Road	TR	981	Old Town Road	TR
884	Buena Vista Road	TR	982	Trail (to possible campground)	TR
887	Old Route 16	TR	984	Whiskey Spring Park Mason-Dixon Trail (8)	P
888	PA 16 (5) (resupply exit)	P	987	Camp Tuckahoe trail	TR
890	Mentzer Gap Road (3)	P	988	White Rock Trail	TR
891	Mentzer Gap Road	TR	993	Gutshall, to P	TR
893	Rattlesnake Run Road	TR	994	Ledigh Road (10)	P
897	Rattlesnake Run Road (4)	P	995	Ledigh Road (5)	P
899	Trail to P (40)	TR	998	(BS) Mountain Road	MU
901	Rattlesnake Run Road (5)	P	999	Butcher Hill Yellow Breeches Cr	MU
903	Old Forge Road (3)	P	1000	(BS) 1st Street, PA 174	MU
904	Trail, unknown	TR	1001	(BS) Butcher Hill Road	MU
905	Snowy Mountain Tower Road (3)	P	1002	(BS) PA 174 E	MU
908	Swamp Road	TR	1003	Trail, unknown	TR
909	Raccoon Run Trail	TR	1004	PA 74	TR
910	PA 233 (3)	P	1005	Lisburn Road (6)	P
913	Access road	TR	1007	PA 641 / Trindle Road (4)	P
914	(CSP) US 30 / Trolley Trail	MU	1009	Ridge Road	TR
915	(CSP) Ramble Trail W	MU	1010	Old Stonehouse Road	TR
916	(CSP) Ramble Trail E	MU	1011	Appalachian Drive	TR
917	(CSP) Bridge / AT / Park Trail	MU	1015	US 11	TR
919	W Parking (Chinquapin) neck	MU	1016	Bernheisel Road (6)	P
920	(CSP) Three Valley Trail	MU	1019	Bernheisel Road (Scott Farm)	TR

HF ATC HQ = Harpers Ferry, Appalachian Trail Conservancy Headquarters Office; ATCH = Appalachian Trail Conservancy Headquarters; TR = trail/road; VC = Visitor Center; HF = Harpers Ferry; P = parking; MU = multiple use; MD = Maryland State Road; PA = Pennsylvania State Road; CSP = Caledonia State Park, PA; AT = Appalachian National Scenic Trail; PGF = Pine Grove Furnace State Park, PA; BS = Boiling Springs, PA.

[a] Numbers in parentheses indicates the number of parking spots.

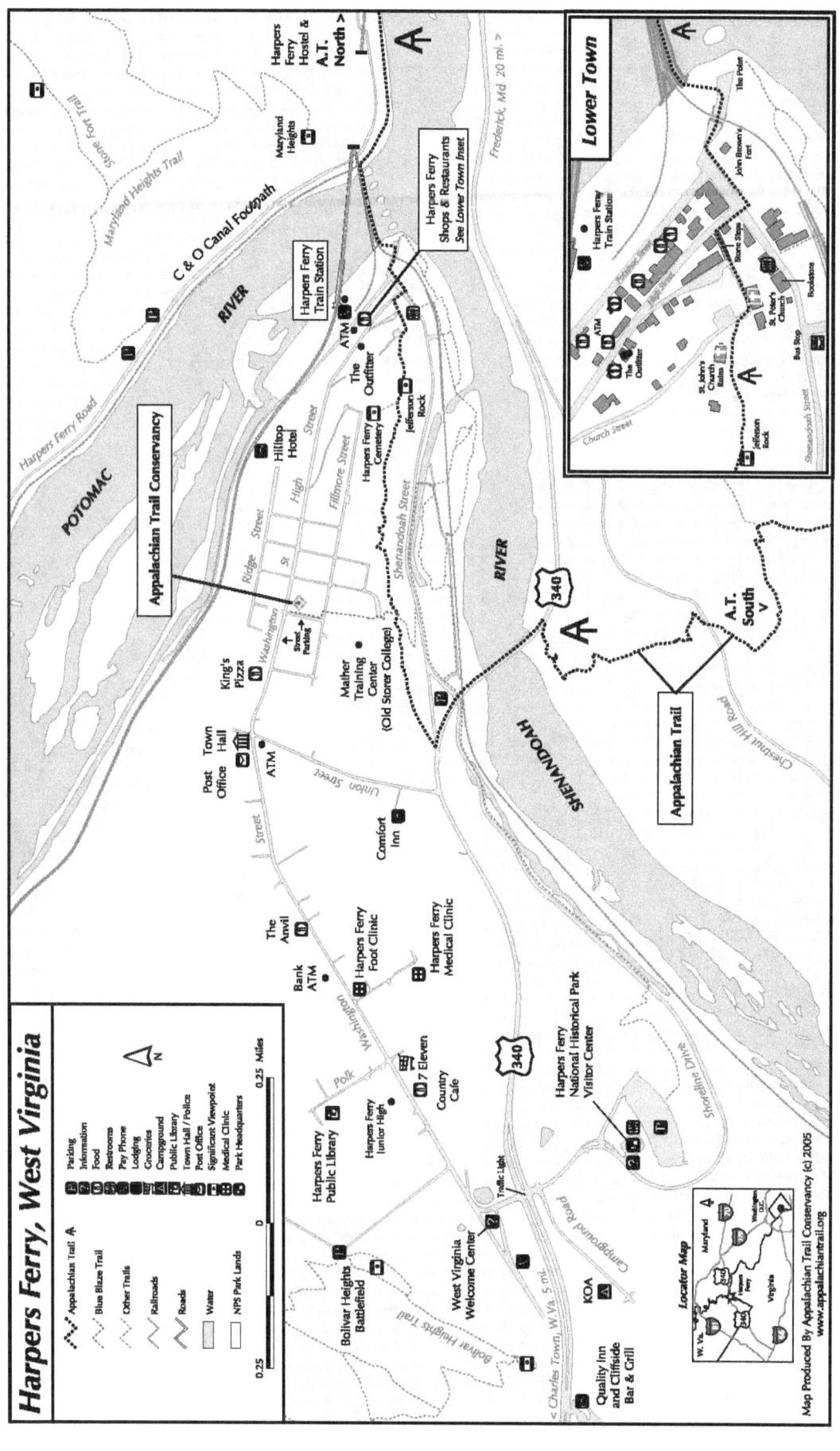

Figure 3 — A map of Harpers Ferry, WV, illustrating the intersection of the Appalachian Trail with the town which leads to the development of the site-type Harpers Ferry.

visitation from Harpers Ferry, WV. This would then bias the visitation estimate for the TR strata if the Mather Side Trail was included in the site-type TR. Second, double counting may result because many people from the Mather Side Trail also visit, and would, thus, be counted at the ATCH site-type. Thirdly, the ATCH site-type had counts for practically the entire year from an auxiliary source which would be more useful than counts from a sample of the Mather Side Trail site days. Thus, the Mather Side Trail will not be discussed or included in any tables, figures, and analyses in the rest of this report. In addition, the special event on June 2 at Boiling Springs, PA, was excluded because it was surveyed in a different manner and included five site days; i.e., all five exit sites within Boiling Springs on June 2. Thus, the total pilot survey sampling frame consisted of 8,995 site days distributed by site-type and use-level as shown in table 2. The TR–L stratum had the most site days, totaling 40 percent of the entire sampling frame. The next largest were P–L with

20 percent and MU–L with 13 percent. Although these strata may represent low-exit volumes and, thus, low levels of daily visitation, they comprise 73 percent of all site days and, therefore, may have a large impact on the visitation estimate.

Standard and augmented sites—The sites identified on the AT are classified as either standard or augmented. The standard sites are those where no information about recreation visitation is available from any sources except the pilot survey itself. In contrast, augmented sites are those where information is available from an auxiliary source that could be used, alone or in conjunction with other information, to derive an estimate of recreation visitation. For example, one might have monthly traffic counts, but would need information on the percentage of vehicles that contained LERs and the average number of people per vehicle to arrive at an estimate of recreation visits. The pilot survey designated all TR, P, and MU

Table 2—The total site days in each of the pilot study strata based on site-type and use-level, the original designed allocation of the sample of site days for a.m. and p.m. sampling (the actual achieved sample days in parentheses), and the total site days for the entire AT[a]

Site-type	Use-level	Pilot survey total	Allocated a.m. sample size (achieved)	Allocated p.m. sample size (achieved)	Allocated sample size total (achieved)	AT total[a]
					number of site days	
TR	L	3,624	4 (4)	6 (8)	10 (12)	184,988
TR	M	651	4 (3)	6 (6)	10 (9)	8,112
TR	H	0	0 (0)	0 (0)	0 (0)	9,490
P	L	1,781	4 (4)	6 (7)	10 (11)	81,429
P	M	689	5 (6)	10 (7)	15 (13)	19,140
P	H	80	9 (8)	16 (12)	25 (20)	8,625
MU	L	1,161	4 (4)	6 (3)	10 (7)	13,279
MU	M	542	5 (5)	10 (10)	15 (15)	3,028
MU	H	167	9 (7)	16 (14)	25 (21)	2,883
HF[b]	L	156	1 (0)	3 (2)	4 (2)	791
HF[b]	M	23	2 (2)	3 (2)	5 (4)	156
HF[b]	H	46	4 (2)	7 (8)	11 (10)	148
ATCH	L	0	0 (0)	0 (0)	0 (0)	120
ATCH	M	14	—[c] —[c]	—[c] —[c]	2 (2)	157
ATCH	H	61	—[c] —[c]	—[c] —[c]	4 (4)	88
Total[d e]		8,995	51 (45)	89 (79)	146 (130)	332,434

AT = Appalachian National Scenic Trail; TR = trail/road; P = parking; MU = multiple use; HF = Harpers Ferry; ATCH = Appalachian Trail Conservancy Headquarters; L = low; M = medium; H = high.
[a] Does not include Foundry Day at Boiling Springs, PA, on June 2, 2007, which included 5 site days.
[b] HF are the sites 810, 811, and 813 at Harpers Ferry, WV.
[c] ATCH was sampled for approximately 7 to 8 hours each day so no a.m. and p.m. is indicated.
[d] Mather Side Trail was originally in the sampling frame, sample calendar, and backup sample but was deleted from all of these.
[e] In the original prework site 881 was site-type MU and the sample calendar was developed from this. However, later the site was reclassified as site-type TR which resulted in two more samples than planned in TR and two less in MU.

7

site-types as standard and the HF and ATCH site-types as augmented.

Generally, it is beneficial to have as many augmented sites as possible because it can increase the efficiency of the survey when using supplemental information collected by other sources. This results in cost savings which allows additional sampling to be allocated to the standard sites, thus, increasing the sample size and reducing variability. In addition, the variances of the estimates associated with augmented sites where data collection is usually more intensive and better controlled are often much less than that of the standard sites, so the quality of the visitation estimates that include augmented sites is further improved.

Although augmented sites can be very advantageous, they may present a few difficulties. First, the identification of augmented sites may be difficult and often requires extensive interaction with field personnel who are familiar with the sites and know which management activities are being performed that may enable the site to be an augmented site. Second, the concept of an augmented site is often a vague and abstract concept that must be understood in order to optimally identify these sites. Third, individual augmented sites may require unique methods of estimation that add complexity to the sampling methodology. Despite these problems, the use of augmented sites has been found to be worth the additional effort in terms of cost savings and variance reduction (English and others 2003).

Prework spreadsheets—The creation of the sampling frame and strata required the identification and strata characterization of all sites along the entire AT. This was initially performed for the pilot survey area and subsequently completed for the rest of the mid-Atlantic region, along with the New England, Virginia, and southern regions. Beginning with Springer Mountain, GA, and continuing to Mount Katahdin, ME, all sites were given a site number, a site name, and assigned a site-type. Overall, a total of 953 "unique" exit sites were identified with 849 being open the entire year.

The formulation of the sampling frame was a vital component of the pilot survey and was dependent on the prework spreadsheets. Data entry consisted of identifying one to several date spans (begin and end) for a given site such that the specified days of the week all had the same use-level as assigned to that date span. A "1" was entered for a day of the week if it had that use-level in the date span and a blank if not. If a holiday had the same use-level, then a "1" was also entered, if not, then a blank (detailed examples follow in the next paragraph). Five recognized holidays were presumed to affect AT visitation—Memorial Day, Independence Day, Labor Day, Columbus Day, and Thanksgiving. Although others like Christmas Day and New Year's Day may attract increased visitation to the AT

by some avid hikers, it was felt that due to possible adverse weather conditions and other social and cultural activities, their impact on AT visitation would not merit holiday status.

Many sites had a simple use patterns. For example, at site number 809 all days of the year were use-level L, so only one date span was needed with "1" for all days of the week and the holiday (app. B). However, others sites had more complex patterns of use-levels. For instance, site number 810 required seven date spans to represent its use-levels. This site had one date span for the time period January 2, 2007, (102) to December 24, 2007, (1224) to represent use-level L for all 5 weekdays. However, two additional date spans were needed for the weekends from January 2, 2007, (102) to March 31, 2007, (331) and November 1, 2007, (1101) to December 24, 2007, (1224) where use-level was M. In addition, January 1, 2007, (101) was considered use-level H, so a separate date span had to be created because this was not one of the specified five holidays. The date span from April 1, 2007, (401) to October 31, 2007, (1031) was specified use-level H for only the weekends, but for December 25, 2007, (1225) to December 31, 2007, (1231) use-level H was given to all days of the week. All five holidays were considered use-level H and, thus, given the date span 101 to 1231 with "1" for holiday only. Note that each holiday could have been specified individually or possibly specified in a previous date span, but for this situation it was simply easier to "bundle" them under one date span. Thus, there are many ways in which the use-levels could be specified for a given site which led to identical classifications for all days of the year.

Although the method presented for site classification may appear confusing at first, once grasped it is simple and efficient for data entry and analysis. To ensure data quality, edit checks were performed to verify that a given site had at most one use-level for a given day and at most only 365 days open for recreation with use-level L, M, or H. Such errors are common, especially for those entering data using this method for the first time. The number of sites identified for each of the regions was New England = 239, mid-Atlantic (excluding pilot) = 319, pilot = 120, Virginia = 146, and southern = 129, for a total of 953. The Mather Side Trail site is not included. The percent of sites open every day of the calendar year for each of the regions was: New England = 67 percent, mid-Atlantic (excluding pilot) = 98 percent, pilot = 99 percent, Virginia = 100 percent, and southern = 86 percent, with the overall weighted average being 89 percent.

The creation of the prework spreadsheet for the site-type ATCH was based on the augmented site data obtained from the Appalachian Trail Conservancy Headquarters (ATCH) Office in Harpers Ferry, WV. According to personnel at the ATCH, their daily tally data consisted of one tally only for each person who came into the ATCH, so multiple enters/exits by the same individual were eliminated. The ATCH staff was obviously not included in the daily tallies. However, a delivery person who showed interest in the AT or asked questions may be included. Months were characterized based on their monthly average visitor tallies with use-level L being < 20, M being 20 to 60, and H being > 60. In certain months, the weekends had significantly higher visitation than their monthly average and, thus, were classified into the next higher use-level. This resulted in January 1, 2007, through March 30, 2007, being use-level L. The period from March 31, 2007, through April 30, 2007, was M on weekdays and H on weekends. All of May 2007 was M on weekdays and H on weekends and Memorial Day. Both June 2007 and July 2007 were H all month while August 2007 and September 2007 were M all month. October 2007 was M on weekdays and H on weekends. November 2007 was M all month while December 2007 was L all month. Appendix B illustrates these data in prework spreadsheet format.

Sample selection—The sampling frame for the pilot survey consisted of 8,995 site days from which 146 sample days were selected randomly within the specified strata according to the sample allocation shown in table 2. Although proportional allocation (Cochran 1977) could have been used to determine the number of site days to sample per stratum, a more efficient method is Neyman (optimal) allocation which selects more site days from the strata that are larger and/or more variable (Cochran 1977). The prework that was done for the creation of the sampling frame provided the information on strata size (table 2). However, although a measure of absolute variability was not known, a relative measure was believed to be positively correlated with use-level, which was found true after sampling was completed. Thus, using the Neyman allocation approach an allocation pattern was created as shown in table 2.

The allocation for the pilot survey relied upon researcher judgment for the optimal way to use the limited labor and financial resources of 146 sample days and, thus, did not strictly follow Neyman allocation. The approach, again requiring considerable researcher judgment, was to get the best sample possible while adhering to the Neyman allocation principles of strata size and variability. All TR site days in all use-levels were believed to have very low visitation and, thus, low variability so all use-levels were assigned 10 site days which was considered the minimum acceptable sample size. The P and MU site days had the opportunity for higher visitation and higher variability, especially for use-levels M and H; so 10, 15, and 25 were allocated to their L, M, and H use-level strata, respectively. Although visitation on the HF site days was anticipated to be very high, there were relatively few site days in these strata, so following the Neyman allocation principles 4, 5, and 11 were assigned to the L, M, and H use-levels,

respectively. Note that this is less than the minimum of 10 due to the limited resources issue and the low strata sample size. The ATCH site consisted of a total of only 75 site days, so only 2 and 4 site days were assigned to M and H, respectively.

The survey design was based on a 6-hour interviewing period for each selected sample site day. Bowker and others (2004) used 4- or 8-hour periods depending on time of year. The USFS uses 6-hour periods for NVUM (English and others 2002, Zarnoch and others 2002). This 6-hour sampling period for the TR, P, MU, and HF site-types was allocated randomly with one-third in the a.m. and two-thirds in the p.m. This disproportionate sampling allocation was used to get a better estimate during the afternoon hours when exiting visitation was believed to be higher and when there would be a greater potential to obtain more interviews and, hence, more survey information. The visitation estimate was weighted accordingly. The ATCH site-type was open for visitation from 9:00 a.m. to 5:00 p.m. (4:00 p.m. on weekends), so the sampling period was not assigned to an a.m. or p.m. category. The sampling calendar (table 3) was developed by randomly selecting the allocated sample size from each stratum by using a custom-designed computer program. Backup sampling days were generated in case the scheduled ones from the sample calendar could not be followed for a variety of reasons, which occasionally occurred as shown in table 3. The sample sizes that were actually achieved for the strata during the pilot survey, accounting for missing sample days and backup substitutes, are shown in table 2.

Characterization of the pilot survey sampling days— There were 146 sampling days scheduled for the pilot study, excluding the special event at Boiling Springs, PA on June 2, 2007. The number of these actually sampled was 114 for a 78.1 percent accomplishment rate. Of the 32 days that were assigned and missed, 12 were completed by using the correct backup days while 2 were completed with ad hoc backup days. In either case, all 14 were of the same site-type and use-level as that of the originally missed sample day, preserving as much as possible the original sampling allocation. Of the 32 missed days, 18 were never replaced with backup days and, thus, the sample size was reduced from what was originally planned. Over the course of the survey, 2 extra sample days were taken—1 was in stratum MU–H and the other in P–L. Thus, the total number of sample days completed by field personnel was 146−18+2 = 130. This consisted of 51 different sites with each being sampled anywhere from 1 to 13 times over the course of the survey. Of this sample, 101 sample days resulted in at least 1 interview being obtained. Although on 29 sample days there were no people observed, and, thus, no interviews, these sample days still provided valuable data because they represented zero visitation.

Table 3—The 2007 pilot survey sample calendar with 146 assigned sampling days along with 2 extra days [this does not include the special event at Boiling Springs, PA (June 2)]

Site	Sub(date) or extra day	Site-type	Use-level	Day	Month	Day	Time	Interviews
816		P	L	Fri.	6	1	a.m.	5
836		P	M	Fri.	6	1	p.m.	4
963		TR	L	Fri.	6	1	p.m.	1
955		MU	H	Sat.	6	2	a.m.	21
921		MU	L	Sat.	6	2	a.m.	0
849	849 (Fri. 6/22)	P	H	Sat.	6	2	a.m.	2
875	849 (Sat. 6/23)	P	H	Sat.	6	2	a.m.	14
955		MU	H	Sun.	6	3	p.m.	28
810		HF	H	Sun.	6	3	p.m.	16
819		P	L	Mon.	6	4	a.m.	1
917		MU	L	Thurs.	6	7	a.m.	1
835		P	L	Thurs.	6	7	a.m.	0
999		MU	H	Sat.	6	9	a.m.	3
875		P	H	Sat.	6	9	a.m.	2
970		P	L	Sat.	6	9	p.m.	0
819		P	H	Sun.	6	10	a.m.	8
849		P	H	Sun.	6	10	p.m.	15
0		ATCH	H	Sun.	6	10	a.m. + p.m.	25
1000		MU	M	Fri.	6	15	p.m.	7
849		P	H	Fri.	6	15	p.m.	11
825		MU	H	Sat.	6	16	a.m.	3
955		MU	H	Sat.	6	16	p.m.	49
1000	1000 (Sat. 6/23)	MU	H	Sat.	6	16	p.m.	12
849		P	H	Sat.	6	16	p.m.	20
832		P	M	Sat.	6	16	p.m.	5
937	849 (Wed. 6/20)	P	M	Sat.	6	16	p.m.	5
810		HF	H	Sat.	6	16	p.m.	18
878		MU	M	Sun.	6	17	a.m.	4
819		P	H	Sun.	6	17	p.m.	6
849		P	H	Sun.	6	17	a.m.	18
841		MU	M	Mon.	6	18	p.m.	0
893		TR	L	Mon.	6	18	p.m.	0
937		P	L	Tues.	6	19	p.m.	1
819		P	L	Wed.	6	20	a.m.	1
825		MU	H	Sat.	6	23	a.m.	2
999		MU	H	Sun.	6	24	p.m.	6
836		P	M	Sun.	6	24	p.m.	—
1000	Extra day	MU	H	Sun.	6	24	p.m.	1
0		ATCH	H	Mon.	6	25	a.m. + p.m.	16
920		MU	L	Tues.	6	26	a.m.	13
994		P	L	Wed.	6	27	p.m.	0
1011		TR	L	Thurs.	6	28	p.m.	0
1015		TR	M	Thurs.	6	28	a.m.	1
878		MU	M	Fri.	6	29	a.m.	5
1000		MU	M	Fri.	6	29	p.m.	7
811		HF	M	Sat.	6	30	a.m.	15
917		MU	M	Sun.	7	1	a.m.	20
819		P	H	Sun.	7	1	a.m.	5
836		P	M	Sun.	7	1	p.m.	4

continued

Table 3—The 2007 pilot survey sample calendar with 146 assigned sampling days along with 2 extra days [this does not include the special event at Boiling Springs, PA (June 2)] (continued)

Site	Sub(date) or extra day	Site-type	Use-level	Day	Month	Day	Time	Interviews
810		HF	H	Sun.	7	1	a.m.	34
813		HF	H	Sun.	7	1	p.m.	40
903		P	L	Mon.	7	2	p.m.	0
811		HF	L	Mon.	7	2	p.m.	35
841		MU	H	Tues.	7	3	a.m.	—
954		MU	M	Wed.	7	4	p.m.	10
849		P	H	Wed.	7	4	p.m.	12
875		P	H	Wed.	7	4	p.m.	0
832	888 (Sun. 8/5)	P	M	Wed.	7	4	p.m.	2
811		HF	M	Wed.	7	4	p.m.	34
923		TR	M	Thurs.	7	5	p.m.	0
999		MU	M	Fri.	7	6	p.m.	6
849		P	H	Fri.	7	6	p.m.	12
949		P	M	Fri.	7	6	a.m.	0
921		MU	L	Sat.	7	7	p.m.	1
999		MU	H	Sun.	7	8	p.m.	6
890		P	M	Sun.	7	8	a.m.	0
813		HF	H	Sun.	7	8	p.m.	58
842		MU	L	Mon.	7	9	p.m.	—
841		MU	H	Tues.	7	10	p.m.	—
901		P	L	Wed.	7	11	p.m.	0
881[a]		TR	L	Thurs.	7	12	p.m.	0
922		MU	L	Thurs.	7	12	p.m.	1
841		MU	H	Sat.	7	14	p.m.	19
919	841 (Thurs. 8/2)	MU	H	Sat.	7	14	p.m.	4
917		MU	M	Sat.	7	14	p.m.	6
819		P	H	Sat.	7	14	p.m.	7
810	813 (Sun. 7/15)	HF	H	Sat.	7	14	a.m.	46
813		HF	H	Sat.	7	14	a.m.	35
811		HF	M	Sat.	7	14	a.m.	20
833		TR	L	Sat.	7	14	p.m.	1
875	875 (Sun. 8/12)	P	H	Sun.	7	15	a.m.	0
865	888 (Wed. 7/11)	P	M	Sun.	7	15	p.m.	1
938		P	M	Sun.	7	15	a.m.	1
811		HF	M	Sun.	7	15	p.m.	41
810		HF	L	Mon.	7	16	p.m.	21
924		TR	M	Mon.	7	16	a.m.	0
841		MU	H	Tues.	7	17	a.m.	2
0		ATCH	H	Tues.	7	17	a.m. + p.m.	7
841		MU	H	Wed.	7	18	p.m.	7
809		TR	L	Wed.	7	18	a.m.	1
881[a]		TR	L	Thurs.	7	19	p.m.	1
934		TR	L	Fri.	7	20	p.m.	0
810		HF	H	Sat.	7	21	p.m.	40
841		MU	H	Sun.	7	22	p.m.	9
919		MU	H	Sun.	7	22	p.m.	—
1002		MU	L	Sun.	7	22	p.m.	25
849	849 (Sun. 7/29)[b]	P	H	Sun.	7	22	p.m.	8
817		TR	L	Sun.	7	22	a.m.	3

continued

11

Table 3—The 2007 pilot survey sample calendar with 146 assigned sampling days along with 2 extra days [this does not include the special event at Boiling Springs, PA (June 2)] (continued)

Site	Sub(date) or extra day	Site-type	Use-level	Day	Month	Day	Time	Interviews
929	930 (Wed. 8/8)	TR	L	Sun.	7	22	a.m.	0
987		TR	M	Mon.	7	23	a.m.	0
841		MU	H	Tues.	7	24	p.m.	12
999		MU	M	Tues.	7	24	p.m.	3
920	920 (Sun. 7/29)[b]	MU	L	Wed.	7	25	a.m.	0
919		MU	M	Wed.	7	25	a.m.	7
849		P	M	Wed.	7	25	a.m.	0
810		HF	L	Thurs.	7	26	a.m.	—
933		TR	M	Fri.	7	27	p.m.	0
1015		TR	M	Fri.	7	27	p.m.	1
819		P	H	Sat.	7	28	p.m.	—
875		P	H	Sat.	7	28	a.m.	25
810		HF	H	Sat.	7	28	p.m.	48
1015		TR	M	Sat.	7	28	p.m.	0
955		MU	H	Sun.	7	29	p.m.	—
875		P	H	Sun.	7	29	p.m.	—
844		P	L	Mon.	7	30	p.m.	1
0		ATCH	H	Mon.	7	30	a.m. + p.m.	11
836		P	M	Wed.	8	1	p.m.	2
875		P	M	Wed.	8	1	p.m.	15
841		MU	H	Fri.	8	3	p.m.	1
838	829 (Mon. 7/16)	TR	L	Fri.	8	3	a.m.	1
927		TR	L	Fri.	8	3	p.m.	0
917		MU	M	Sat.	8	4	p.m.	18
819		P	H	Sat.	8	4	p.m.	—
875		P	H	Sat.	8	4	p.m.	2
950		P	M	Sat.	8	4	a.m.	1
811		HF	M	Sat.	8	4	p.m.	—
925	933 (Tues. 8/7)	TR	M	Sat.	8	4	p.m.	0
878		MU	M	Sun.	8	5	p.m.	7
819		P	H	Sun.	8	5	a.m.	—
849		P	H	Sun.	8	5	p.m.	8
875		P	H	Sun.	8	5	p.m.	—
813		HF	H	Sun.	8	5	a.m.	—
963		TR	M	Mon.	8	6	p.m.	0
938	Extra day	P	L	Mon.	8	6	p.m.	0
0		ATCH	M	Mon.	8	6	a.m. + p.m.	3
841		MU	H	Tues.	8	7	a.m.	—
811		HF	L	Tues.	8	7	p.m.	—
0		ATCH	M	Tues.	8	7	a.m. + p.m.	16
841		MU	H	Wed.	8	8	a.m.	6
955		MU	M	Thurs.	8	9	a.m.	1
841		MU	H	Sat.	8	11	a.m.	5
919		MU	H	Sat.	8	11	p.m.	2
899		TR	M	Sat.	8	11	a.m.	—
849		P	H	Sun.	8	12	p.m.	30
905		P	M	Sun.	8	12	p.m.	—
813		HF	H	Sun.	8	12	p.m.	50
919		MU	M	Mon.	8	13	p.m.	0
841		MU	H	Tues.	8	14	p.m.	0

— = If interviews are missing, then this scheduled sample day was missed; P = parking; TR = trail/road; MU = multiple use; HF = Harpers Ferry; ATCH = Appalachian Trail Conservancy Headquarters; L = low; M = medium; H = high.

[a] Was originally site-type MU but was later reclassified as site-type TR.

[b] Not an official backup day but the site-type and use-level were appropriate.

The major reason for the missing sample days was limited resources available for field survey administration. The pilot study employed two full-time field surveyors and occasionally augmented them with two project surveyors (whose major responsibilities were other duties besides field surveying) and several volunteers. Many of the missed sample days were on days when the number of randomly selected sample days exceeded two and there were insufficient interviewers available to perform the surveys.

Survey procedures—The actual implementation of the survey began with assigning each sample day to a trained field survey interviewer who performed the survey. The procedure consisted of a 6-hour onsite tally of all people that were potential recreationists who appeared to be exiting the site. Obvious nonrecreating people such as uniformed State and Federal park personnel were not included in the survey tally. As mentioned previously, the survey was scheduled to be either a.m. (8:00 to 2:00) or p.m. (2:00 to 8:00) but minor departures from the specific times occurred and were recorded and adjusted for appropriately. At eight of the MU sites exiting vehicles were tallied because the volume and nature of the exiting people were not conducive to a people tally.

In addition, survey interviews were conducted on a random sample of groups that were exiting. The person interviewed was selected randomly from each group by asking which group member, aged 16 or older, had the most recent birthday. The goal was to interview as many groups as possible. Thus, at the use-level L strata all groups may have been interviewed while at the use-level H strata the sampling fraction may have been much lower. The main objective of the questionnaire was to interview only people who appeared to be using the AT for recreation and were leaving the AT for the day at the time of the interview. Exceptions to the exiting criterion occurred at augmented sites like Harpers Ferry and the ATCH, where interviews were at random. All interviewees were screened out with a series of initial questions and then asked another set of questions dealing with arrival time, hiking distance, frequency of previous visits, demographics, and a few other trip attributes (fig. 4). In addition, other people who did not meet these criteria were also interviewed to a limited extent to gather other information needed for the survey estimation process. The exiting people tally during the interviewing period was recorded which provided information on the distribution of exiting people throughout the survey day. At the completion of a survey day, the interviewer filled out the day summary form (fig. 5) which contains information on the interview team, date and time of the survey, tally, and number of completed interviews.

Estimation Methodology

Statistical background—The estimation methodology used to obtain estimates for the pilot survey requires a fundamental knowledge of several statistical concepts. The estimators for visitation are relatively straightforward; however, the computation of variances is usually not. In particular, the sampling design must be considered when computing variances of certain estimated calibrating parameters and quantities. Moreover, visitation estimators often consist of the product or ratio of other estimated variables, and their variances are complex equations. A general introduction to these statistical issues (Cochran 1977) is presented here.

The pilot survey is a complex stratified cluster sampling design that must be considered when obtaining variances of estimated quantities. The primary sampling unit (PSU) is the site day within a stratum and the secondary sampling unit (SSU) is the group interviewed on a given site day. If Y is a variable measured at the PSU level, then an estimator for the mean for a given stratum is the simple arithmetic mean

$$\bar{y} = \frac{1}{n}\sum_{i=1}^{n} y_i \qquad (1)$$

where

y_i = the observed variable on sample day i

n = number of sample days

An estimator for the variance (ignoring the finite population correction) is

$$\hat{V}(\bar{y}) = \frac{\sum_{i=1}^{n}(y_i - \bar{y})^2}{n(n-1)} \qquad (2)$$

When quantities are estimated at the SSU level, the clustering of the data within a sample day must be considered. If this is not done and the observations are viewed as a simple random sample and equations (1) and (2) used, then variances will usually be underestimated, standard errors will be too small, confidence intervals will be too narrow, and statistical tests will have inflated type I error rates. In such a situation, the ratio of means estimator should be used for clustered data and is defined as

Date: ___ / ___ / 2007 Site # ATC Type M / HF Site Name:

_____

Q1:   **Hi. We are conducting a study for the National Park Service. Would you be willing to take a few minutes to participate in an interview?**

      _____ Yes (person agreed to be interviewed – read Introduction)

      _____ No (did not agree to be interviewed – politely stop interview and visually obtain answers to Q 10, 11, 19)

If in group: "**I need to select just one of you to complete this interview. To make sure the survey is random, which of you had the most recent birthday and is 16 or older?**"

(Direct all questions to this person) **"Please take a moment and review the following information."** Important- Allow interviewee to read OMB Information.

Q1.4: **Did you arrive here via the Blue Blaze / Mather Side Trail?**   _____ Yes

(ATC)   _____ No

Jf at Special Site / M (Q1.5 only):

Q1.5: **Did you use the Appalachian Trail today?**
    _____ Yes (continue to Q2)
    _____ No "We are only surveying people who are using the Appalachian Trail. Thank you for your time." (visually obtain Q 10, 11, 19)

Figure 4—The survey questionnaire used to record information for each interviewed person on a sample day. An additional question (1.4) was only asked when sampling at the Appalachian Trail Conservancy. (continued to next page)

Q2. **Is the AT your primary or secondary reason for visiting this area today?**

Primary _____   Secondary _____

Q3: **Is the purpose of your visit to the Appalachian Trail for recreation?**

_____ Yes, recreation type answer   (ex. hiking, bird-watching, etc. continue to Q4)

_____ No, non-recreation (maintainer, volunteer, etc.) "We are only surveying people who

are here for recreation. Thank you for your time." (visually obtain Q 10, 11, 19)

Q4: **Are you leaving the AT for the day, OR will you return and continue on today?**

_____ Leaving the AT for the day (continue to Q4)

_____ Will return and continue on today "We are only surveying people who are exiting

for the last time today. Thank you for your time." (visually obtain Q 10, 11, 19)

Q5: **How did you arrive at the AT today?**

Read: Personal vehicle _____   Bus_____   Bicycle _____   Walking _____

Other _____

Q6: **When did you arrive at the AT for this visit?**

_____ Today: **What Time?** _____ (24 hr.)

_____ Earlier: **When?** Date: _____ / _____ / 2007 & Time: _____ (24 hr.)

Q7: **About how far did you hike on the AT today?**

1 mile or less _____   More than 1 but less than 5 miles _____

5 or more but less than 10 miles _____   10 or more miles _____

Figure 4 (continued)—The survey questionnaire used to record information for each interviewed person on a sample day. An additional question (1.4) was only asked when sampling at the Appalachian Trail Conservancy. (continued to next page)

Q8: **Not including this visit, about how many times have you visited this particular AT site for recreation in the past 12 months?** _____

Q9: **Not including this visit, about how many times have you visited anywhere along the AT for recreation in the past 12 months?** _____

Q10: **How many males and females are in your group today?**

Male: _____ Female: _____

Q11: **How many of those are less than 16 years old?** Male: _____ Female: _____

Q12: **How many continuous nights before today did you stay on the AT?** _____

Q13: **On a scale of 1-10, with 10 being the most satisfied, how satisfied were you with this visit to the Appalachian Trail?** _____

Q14: **On a scale of 1 – 9, with 9 being extremely crowded and 1 being Not at All Crowded, how crowded did you feel on the Appalachian Trail on this trip?** (circle one #)

Not at all Crowded | Slightly Crowded | Moderately Crowded | Extremely Crowded

1   2   3   4   5   6   7   8   9

Q15: **If you could ask Managers to improve <u>one thing</u> about the way people experience the Appalachian Trail, what would you ask them to do?**

_____

Figure 4 (continued)—The survey questionnaire used to record information for each interviewed person on a sample day. An additional question (1.4) was only asked when sampling at the Appalachian Trail Conservancy. (continued to next page)

Q16: **Consider the food, fuel, lodging, equipment and other expenditures necessary for this visit. About how much did your group spend in total for this visit to the A.T?**

(Note: "If your trip involves visits to multiple places, estimate only the share of spending for this visit to the AT") $ _____

Q17: **What is your home Zip Code?** _____ (*99999 if foreign*)

Q18: **What is your age group?** 16-20   21-30   31-40   41-50   51-60   61-70   71+

Q19: **What is your Gender?** M / F

Q20: **Are you Hispanic or Latino(a)?**

No_____   Yes_____   (Refused) _____

Q21: **With which racial group(s) do you most closely identify? Please choose one or more.**

_____ American Indian / Alaska Native

_____ Asian

_____ Black / African American

_____ Native Hawaiian or other Pacific Islander

_____ White

Clicker count (including this interview):_____

_____ (Refused)   End Interview Time: _____ (24 hr.)

Figure 4 (continued) —The survey questionnaire used to record information for each interviewed person on a sample day. An additional question (1.4) was only asked when sampling at the Appalachian Trail Conservancy.

Appalachian Trail Visitor Use Study

Interview Day Summary Form

Complete this form at the end of the interview period.

Interview Team

      Person conducting Interviews: _____

      Person using clicker: _____

Date and Times

      Date: ____/____/_2007_ Weather Conditions: _____

      Site # _____   Site name: _____

      Time at start of interview period: _____ (military)

      Time at end of interview period: _____ (military)

      Scheduled shift: 8 – 2 (Am) or 2 – 8 (Pm)

      Break time (in minutes): _____

Figure 5—The day summary form used to record information for each sample day. (continued to next page)

Is this a Substitute Sample Day?   Yes   No

If so, what was the Original site number / day? #_____ ___/___/___07

Daily Clicker Counts

Total clicker / tally count at the **end** of interview period: _____

Did you count:

_____ Exiting Hikers   **or**   _____Vehicles

(Vehicles are counted at sites 825, 828, 840, 841, 878, 919, 955 and 999)

Index Estimate

Number of vehicles in parking lot: Shift Start_____   Shift End _____

Completed Interviews

Total Number of Surveys Completed at **end** of interview period: _____

Figure 5 (continued)—The day summary form used to record information for each sample day.

$$\hat{R} = \frac{\sum_{i=1}^{n} y_i}{\sum_{i=1}^{n} x_i} = \frac{\bar{y}}{\bar{x}} \qquad (3)$$

where

y_i = the sum of the observed variable for all observations in cluster i

x_i = the number of observations in cluster i

n = number of clusters sampled

The estimated variance (ignoring the finite population correction) is

$$\hat{V}(\hat{R}) = \frac{1}{n(n-1)(\bar{x})^2} \left(\sum_{i=1}^{n} y_i^2 + \hat{R}^2 \sum_{i=1}^{n} x_i^2 - 2\hat{R} \sum_{i=1}^{n} y_i x_i \right) \qquad (4)$$

A couple general variance calculating methods are used quite often in the pilot survey. One is the variance of the product of a constant k and a variable. In this situation

$$\hat{Q}_1 = k\hat{x} \qquad (5)$$

and the estimated variance is

$$\hat{V}(\hat{Q}_1) = k^2 \hat{V}(\hat{x}) \qquad (6)$$

The other is the estimated variance of the sum of two independent estimates

$$\hat{Q}_2 = \hat{x} + \hat{y} \qquad (7)$$

which is simply the sum of the estimated variances of each and is defined as

$$\hat{V}(\hat{Q}_2) = \hat{V}(\hat{x}) \quad \hat{V}(\hat{y}) \qquad (8)$$

Another complexity that is often encountered is the estimated variance for an estimate that is a product of several other estimates that are independent. Let the estimate be defined as the product of two estimated independent quantities as

$$\hat{Q} = \hat{x}\hat{y} \qquad (9)$$

An estimate of the variance (Goodman 1960) is

$$\hat{V}(\hat{Q}_3) = \hat{x}^2 \hat{V}(\hat{y}) + \hat{y}^2 \hat{V}(\hat{x}) - \hat{V}(\hat{x})\hat{V}(\hat{y}) \qquad (10)$$

An extension to the product of three independent variables

$$\hat{Q}_4 = \hat{x}\hat{y}\hat{z} \qquad (11)$$

is often needed and this could be derived as an extension of equation (10) as

$$\begin{aligned} \hat{V}(\hat{Q}_4) = &\ \hat{x}^2\hat{y}^2\hat{V}(\hat{z}) + \hat{x}^2\hat{z}^2\hat{V}(\hat{y}) + \hat{y}^2\hat{z}^2\hat{V}(\hat{x}) \\ &- \hat{x}^2\hat{V}(\hat{y})\hat{V}(\hat{z}) - \hat{y}^2\hat{V}(\hat{x})\hat{V}(\hat{z}) \\ &- \hat{z}^2\hat{V}(\hat{x})\hat{V}(\hat{y}) + \hat{V}(\hat{x})\hat{V}(\hat{y})\hat{V}(\hat{z}) \end{aligned} \qquad (12)$$

Occasionally an estimator is the product of three independent variables, one of which is also a quotient of two independent variables where the denominator is correlated with one of the other product variables. This is an extremely complex situation. When this occurs in the pilot survey, the variance of the quotient variable is very small; thus, it is assumed to be a constant with zero variance. This then reduces to the variance of a product of two variables as in equation (9) and, thus, the variance is estimated using a slight modification of equation (10).

Two approaches were used for estimating the various calibration parameters for the visitation estimators in the strata. The design-based estimation approach is the traditional methodology where estimators are developed from the sample data from each stratum according to a cluster survey design as outlined in statistical references such as Cochran (1977). This is the optimal method provided sufficient sample data have been obtained. However, when resources are limited, as was the case in the pilot survey, a model-based estimation approach may be more appropriate.

In the current study, a mixed linear model is developed by pooling the data from all the strata. The fixed components of the model are site-type and use-level. The interaction is assumed negligible and, thus, excluded from the model. The clustering of the observations within the sample days is addressed by treating them as repeated measures with the variance components covariance structure, implying a common variance and zero covariance for the observations within a cluster. The estimated parameters from the model are used to obtain the strata means and variances which reflect a smoother relationship than those from the design-based approach. When sample size is small and the data is highly variable, this is an appealing property. The assumption of no interaction between site-type and use-level seems reasonable and is a necessary tradeoff for the smoother relationship. When the assumption is not valid, then the design-based approach may be more appropriate. If interaction effects are put into the model, then the estimates are identical to the design-based approach, though the variances are slightly different.

Another advantage of the model-based approach is that it is possible to obtain estimates for strata that are not specifically represented in the sample data as long as their site-type and use-level are represented in the data. In this situation the design-based approach would have to use a more arbitrary method to obtain a pooled estimate. This is not a factor for the pilot survey because all 13 strata were represented with data, and both approaches may be used. However, the TWE required estimates for two strata that were not represented with the pilot survey data which gives additional support to using the model-based approach. Moreover, the model-based approach has the potential to yield smaller variances because the estimates are based on data from all strata and not just one stratum as in the design-based approach. Thus, for these reasons, the pilot survey examined both approaches and after evaluation, used the model-based approach for the final estimates.

Pilot survey visitation estimator—Total visitation for the pilot survey from June 1 to August 14, 2007, is defined as

$$VISITS = SS + AS + SE \qquad (13)$$

where

VISITS = the total number of recreation visits to the AT in the pilot study area from June 1 through August 14, 2007

SS = the total number of AT standard site visits

AS = the total number of AT augmented site visits

SE = the total number of AT recreation visits from the special event sites at Boiling Springs, PA, on June 2, 2007

The determination of an LER was dependent on the site-type of the sample day. For site-types TR and P, any potential interviewee who refused to be interviewed was considered an LER. In contrast, for site-types MU, ATCH, and HF, a refusal was simply considered a missing observation. The rationale for this was that it was believed that refusals at site-types TR and P were most likely LERs because these site-types were generally in remote areas with few other activities besides hiking on the AT. However, at site-types MU, ATCH, and HF there was a much higher diversity of activities and the likelihood of being an LER or non-LER was indeterminate.

All three components are independent so the variance is

$$\hat{V}\left(VISITS\right) = \hat{V}\left(\hat{SS}\right) + \hat{V}\left(\hat{AS}\right) + \hat{V}\left(\hat{SE}\right) \qquad (14)$$

Each of the above three components requires a different estimation methodology which is now presented.

Standard site-type component—The standard site-type component consisted of all sites in the strata composed of the TR, P, and MU site-types and all three use-levels L, M, and H where they existed. The standard site-type component, which does not contain the TR–H stratum in the pilot survey, is estimated as

$$\hat{SS} = \sum_{h=1}^{8} N_h \overline{P}_h \overline{C}_h \overline{G}_h \qquad (15)$$

with estimated variance

$$
\begin{aligned}
\hat{V}\left(\hat{SS}\right) = &\sum_{h=1}^{8} N_h^2 \left\{ \overline{P}_h^2 \overline{C}_h^2 \hat{V}\left(\overline{G}_h\right) + \overline{P}_h^2 \overline{G}_h^2 \hat{V}\left(\overline{C}_h\right) \right. \\
&\left. + \overline{C}_h^2 \overline{G}_h^2 \hat{V}\left(\overline{P}_h\right) \right\} \\
&- \sum_{h=1}^{8} N_h^2 \left\{ \overline{P}_h^2 \hat{V}\left(\overline{C}_h\right) \hat{V}\left(\overline{G}_h\right) + \overline{C}_h^2 \hat{V}\left(\overline{P}_h\right) \hat{V}\left(\overline{G}_h\right) \right. \\
&\left. + \overline{G}_h^2 \hat{V}\left(\overline{P}_h\right) \hat{V}\left(\overline{C}_h\right) \right\} \\
&+ \sum_{h=1}^{8} N_h^2 \hat{V}\left(\overline{P}_h\right) \hat{V}\left(\overline{C}_h\right) \hat{V}\left(\overline{G}_h\right)
\end{aligned}
\qquad (16)
$$

where

N_h = the total number of site days in stratum h

$\overline{P}_h$ = the average proportion of exiting groups in stratum h that are LERs

$\overline{C}_h$ = the average number of groups of people (recreating or not) counted as exiting in stratum h

$\overline{G}_h$ = the average size of the LER group in stratum h

$\hat{V}(\overline{P}_h), \hat{V}(\overline{C}_h),$ and $\hat{V}(\overline{G}_h)$ = the estimated variances of $\overline{P}_h, \overline{C}_h,$ and $\overline{G}_h,$ respectively

Note that the index of summation does not include strata TR–H because it does not exist in the pilot survey and, thus, there are only eight strata.

To get an estimate for equation (15), each of the four components must be obtained and multiplied. The N_h are known constants and are obtained from the prework spreadsheet data (table 2) while the $\overline{P}_h, \overline{C}_h,$ and $\overline{G}_h$ are estimated from the interview survey data.

Let

n_h = the number of sample days in stratum h

m_{hi} = number of groups interviewed on sample day i in stratum h

P_{hij} = 1 if group j on sample day i in stratum h was an LER
= 0 elsewhere

Moreover, there are two types of groups that are recognized in the interview process—those that are LER and those that are not. Thus,

Let

g_{hij} = the number of people in interview group j on sample day i in stratum h for an LER group

g_{hij}^a = the number of people in interview group j on sample day i in stratum h for any type of group (the superscript "a" refers to "all" groups)

Also, there are two types of site days—those which tally people and those which tally vehicles.

Let

c_{hi}^p = the number of people tallied exiting the AT from sample day i in stratum h during the 6-hour interview period

c_{hi}^v = the number of vehicles tallied exiting the AT from sample day i in stratum h during the 6-hour interview period

The survey data can be used to obtain a ratio-of-means estimator for $\overline{P}_h$ defined as

$$\overline{P}_h = \frac{\sum_{i=1}^{n_h}\sum_{j=1}^{m_{hi}} p_{hij}}{\sum_{i=1}^{n_h} m_{hi}} \qquad (17)$$

with estimated variance

$$\hat{V}(\overline{P}_h) = \frac{1}{n_h(n_h-1)\left(\frac{1}{n_h}\sum_{i=1}^{n_h} m_{hi}\right)^2}\left\{\sum_{i=1}^{n_h}\left(\sum_{j=1}^{m_{hi}} p_{hij}\right)^2\right.$$
$$\left. + \overline{P}_h^2 \sum_{i=1}^{n_h} m_{hi}^2 - 2\overline{P}_h \sum_{i=1}^{n_h}\left(m_{hi}\sum_{j=1}^{m_{hi}} p_{hij}\right)\right\} \qquad (18)$$

This estimator considers the clustering of the data on a site-day basis. The estimators given in equations (17) and (18) are valid when the number of sample days in a stratum is evenly distributed in the a.m. and p.m. categories. However, as the sample allocation was one-third a.m. and two-thirds p.m., an appropriate weighting scheme was used. In addition, missed sampling days and sample days without interviews (and no p_{hij}) further distort the designed allocation. Thus, the weights used for a given stratum were obtained as the proportion of sample days containing at least one p_{hij} that were a.m. and p.m. For instance, in stratum P–H the original allocation was a.m. = 9 and p.m. = 16 but the achieved was a.m. = 8 and p.m. = 12 with the number of sample days with at least one p_{hij} being a.m. = 7 and p.m. = 11. Thus, the weights used for stratum P–H were a.m. = 7/18 = 0.39 and p.m. = 11/18 = 0.61. The analytical equations based on these weights are quite complicated and will not be presented here. Practical calculation of these estimators was easily performed for the design-based and model-based approaches by using PROC SURVEYMEANS and PROC MIXED (SAS Institute Inc. 2004), respectively.

To obtain the average daily tally $\overline{C}_h$, the arithmetic mean is used because the daily count data are not clustered. Thus, when the sample day is a vehicle tally,

$$\overline{C}_h = \frac{\sum_{i=1}^{n_h} 2c_{hi}^v}{n_h} \qquad (19)$$

with variance

$$\hat{V}\left(\overline{C}_h\right) = \frac{4\sum_{i=1}^{n_h}\left(c_{hi}^v - \overline{c}_h^v\right)^2}{n_h\left(n_h - 1\right)} \qquad (20)$$

The estimators shown in equations (19) and (20) are valid when the number of sample days in a stratum is evenly distributed in the a.m. and p.m. categories. This was not the case in the pilot survey, so separate estimates for a stratum were computed for a.m. and p.m. using equations (19) and (20). The a.m. and p.m. were then combined by simply averaging which achieved the appropriate weighting and the variance was computed in the typical manner.

The constant "2" in equation (19) expands the 6-hour tally to a 12-hour recreation day. Note that for the TWE no adjustment is used to calibrate the recreation day to a shorter length during the winter months. This is because the use-level for a site was defined on a day basis. However, if the use-level was on a density-per-hour basis then a day length adjustment would be needed.

Recall that at a specific site either people or vehicles may be tallied as outlined in the sampling protocol. Although only eight sites are vehicle tally sites and the others are people tally sites, the survey is based on interviewing groups and, thus, vehicle tallies are the appropriate unit. This is because the group is the sampling unit for the interviews but the tally of groups may be impossible to accurately obtain if noninterviewed groups that pass the survey spot are attempted to be tallied. For vehicle sites the group is easily tallied because it is contained in a vehicle. At people sites exiting groups of people may mix together causing tally problems. Therefore, it is imperative to convert all people tally sample days to vehicle tally days before using the estimator (19) and its variance (20). This conversion is defined as

$$c_{hi}^v = \frac{c_{hi}^p}{\sum_{j=1}^{m_{hi}} \dfrac{g_{hij}^a}{m_{hi}}} \qquad (21)$$

In addition, note that the denominator in equation (21) is the average group size for all exiting groups for a specific day i in stratum h, which is used to convert the people count c_{hi}^p to a vehicle count c_{hi}^v. This is performed on a sample day basis and yields the variable c_{hi}^v directly from which the stratum mean and variance could be easily obtained using equations (1) and (2), respectively. This is

preferred to using the average exiting all group size for the entire stratum in the denominator of equation (21) in which case the variable c_{hi}^v would be a ratio of two variables. To obtain the variance of such a variable would require a more complicated equation that would include the covariance of the numerator and denominator.

To obtain an estimator for group size, the ratio-of-means must again be used for clustered data, yielding

$$\overline{G}_h = \frac{\sum_{i=1}^{n_h}\sum_{j=1}^{m_{hi}} g_{hij}}{\sum_{i=1}^{n_h} m_{hi}} \qquad (22)$$

with estimated variance

$$\hat{V}\left(\overline{G}_h\right) = \frac{1}{n_h\left(n_h - 1\right)\left(\dfrac{1}{n_h}\sum_{i=1}^{n_h} m_{hi}\right)^2} \left\{ \sum_{i=1}^{n_h}\left(\sum_{j=1}^{m_{hi}} g_{hij}\right)^2 \right.$$
$$\left. + \overline{G}_h^2 \sum_{i=1}^{n_h} m_{hi}^2 - 2\overline{G}_h \sum_{i=1}^{n_h}\left(m_{hi}\sum_{j=1}^{m_{hi}} g_{hij}\right) \right\} \qquad (23)$$

The estimators shown in equations (22) and (23) are valid when the number of sample days in a stratum is evenly distributed between the a.m. and p.m. categories. However, as mentioned previously, the sample allocation was one-third a.m. and two-thirds p.m., and this has to be taken into account by appropriate weighting in the estimation process. In addition, missed sampling days and sample days without interviews (and no g_{hij}) further distort the designed allocation. Thus, the weights used for a given stratum were obtained as the proportion of sample days containing at least one g_{hij} that were a.m. and p.m. Thus, the weighting methodology described for $\overline{P}_h$ was also used here.

The standard site-type estimator equation (15) is obtained by substituting the quantities for N_h, $\overline{P}_h$ from equation (17), $\overline{C}_h$ from equation (19), and $\overline{G}_h$ from equation (22) into equation (15). The estimated variance is found by substituting the corresponding variances from equations (18), (20), and (23) into equation (16).

Augmented site-type component—*Site-type ATCH*—The site-type ATCH augmented site data consisted of 75 daily visitor tallies at the ATCH Office in Harpers Ferry, WV, obtained from June 1 through August 14, 2007. This was combined with the estimates $\overline{P}_h$ and $\overline{G}_h$ obtained from the 6 sample site days taken during the pilot survey at the ATCH.

The ATCH was open for 8 hours during the week and 7 hours on weekends which was considered the entire day with respect to last exiting recreationists. Thus, no adjustment for day length of 7 or 8 hours or expansion to a 12-hour day was used.

The visitation estimate for the ATCH for the pilot survey is as follows.

Let

N_h = total number of days that the ATCH has days in use-level h, $(h=M,H)$, during the pilot survey

n_h = number of days the ATCH tallied visitors for stratum h, during the pilot survey

AS_{hi}^{ATCH} = the ATCH visitor tally on day i in use-level h

then, the average daily augmented site-type visitation tally in use-level h is the arithmetic mean

$$\overline{AS_h^{ATCH}} = \frac{\sum_{i=1}^{n_h} AS_{hi}^{ATCH}}{n_h} \qquad (24)$$

with estimated variance

$$\hat{V}\left(\overline{AS_h^{ATCH}}\right) = \left(1 - \frac{n_h}{N_h}\right) \frac{\sum_{i=1}^{n_h} \left(AS_{hi}^{ATCH} - \overline{AS_h^{ATCH}}\right)^2}{n_h(n_h - 1)} = 0 \quad (25)$$

Note that all 75 days were tallied and, thus, $N_h = n_h = 75$ and consequently the finite population correction is zero which results in the variance being equal to zero.

The visitation estimate for the ATCH for the pilot survey is defined as

$$AS^{ATCH} = \sum_{h=M}^{H} N_h \overline{P}_h \left(\frac{\overline{AS_h^{ATCH}}}{\overline{G_h^a}}\right) \overline{G}_h \qquad (26)$$

where

AS^{ATCH} = total visitation estimate for the ATCH for the pilot survey

$\overline{P}_h$ = the proportion of groups exiting the ATCH that are AT LER

$\overline{G_h^a}$ = the average group size for all groups exiting the ATCH

$\overline{G}_h$ = the average group size for all AT LER groups exiting the ATCH

The $\overline{P}_h$ and $\overline{G}_h$ are estimated as described previously in equations (17) and (22) and $\overline{G_h^a}$ is estimated in a similar ratio-of-means manner as

$$\overline{G_h^a} = \frac{\sum_{i=1}^{n_h} \sum_{j=1}^{m_{hi}} g_{hij}^a}{\sum_{i=1}^{n_h} m_{hi}} \qquad (27)$$

with estimated variance

$$\hat{V}\left(\overline{G_h^a}\right) = \frac{1}{n_h(n_h-1)\left(\frac{1}{n_h}\sum_{i=1}^{n_h} m_{hi}\right)^2} \left\{\sum_{i=1}^{n_h}\left(\sum_{j=1}^{m_{hi}} g_{hij}^a\right)^2 \right.$$
$$\left. + \overline{G_h^a}^2 \sum_{i=1}^{n_h} m_{hi}^2 - 2\overline{G_h^a} \sum_{i=1}^{n_h}\left(m_{hi}\sum_{j=1}^{m_{hi}} g_{hij}^a\right)\right\} \qquad (28)$$

where

g_{hij}^a = the number of people in interview group j on sample day i in stratum h for any type of group

m_{hi} = number of groups interviewed on sample day i in stratum h

Note that in equation (26) the summation is only over the use-levels M and H.

The estimators given in equations (27) and (28) are valid when the number of sample days in a stratum is evenly distributed in the a.m. and p.m. categories. However, as mentioned previously, the sample allocation was one-third a.m. and two-thirds p.m., and this has to be taken into account by appropriate weighting in the estimation process. In addition, missed sampling days and sample days without interviews (and no g_{hij}^a) further distort the designed allocation. Thus, the weights used for a given stratum were obtained as the proportion of sample days containing at least one g_{hij}^a that were a.m. and p.m. Thus, the weighting methodology described for $\overline{P}_h$ was also used here.

The variance of estimator (26) is quite complicated because it is a product of a constant and three variables as well as a ratio of a dependent variable. To simplify matters, assume that $\overline{G_h^a}$ is a constant, which is reasonable because its variance is quite small and it is highly correlated with $\overline{G}_h$. Then we have approximately

$$\hat{V}\left(AS^{ATCH}\right) = \sum_{h=M}^{H} N_h^2 \left(\overline{\frac{AS_h^{ATCH}}{\hat{G}_h^a}}\right)^2 \left\{\overline{P}_h^2 \hat{V}\left(\overline{G}_h\right) \right.$$
$$\left. + \overline{G}_h^2 \hat{V}\left(\overline{P}_h\right) - \hat{V}\left(\overline{P}_h\right)\hat{V}\left(\overline{G}_h\right)\right\} \quad (29)$$

because $\hat{V}\left(\overline{AS^{ATCH}}\right) = 0$ as shown in equation (25) which drops four terms out of the general variance equation (12), simplifying the variance to a product of only two variables and two constants.

Augmented site-type component—*Site-type HF*—The HF site-type consisted of the three sites located at Harpers Ferry (810, 811, and 813). Although these sites could have been sampled and visitation estimated similarly to the standard sites, it was more advantageous to utilize the official monthly NPS recreation visitation for Harpers Ferry National Historical Park as augmented site data[1] (National Park Service 2008). This provided visitation estimates based on data for the total 75 days at Harpers Ferry which was considered superior to just visitation estimates derived from the 20 site days that were planned to be sampled by the pilot study. In addition, it provided data for the entire year which was also advantageous for the TWE. However, there were several limitations to using this augmented site data that had to be resolved. The reported NPS visitation included (a) both AT and non-AT visits, (b) was not stratified by use-level, and (c) was only available on a monthly basis. To resolve these problems required a monthly $\overline{P}_i$ derived from weighting the individual three use-level estimates obtained from the pilot study for the site-type HF by the monthly strata weights obtained from the prework spreadsheet data. The weighted $\overline{P}_i$ and variance were defined as

$$\overline{P}_i = \frac{N_{Li}\overline{P}_L + N_{Mi}\overline{P}_M + N_{Hi}\overline{P}_H}{N_{Li} + N_{Mi} + N_{Hi}} \quad (30)$$

$$\hat{V}\left(\overline{P}_i\right) = \frac{N_{Li}^2\hat{V}\left(\overline{P}_L\right) + N_{Mi}^2\hat{V}\left(\overline{P}_M\right) + N_{Hi}^2\hat{V}\left(\overline{P}_H\right)}{N_{Li} + N_{Mi} + N_{Hi}^2} \quad (31)$$

[1] Personal communication. 2008. Butch Street, Management analyst, U.S. Department of the Interior, National Park Service, Public Use Statistics Office, Denver, CO 80225.

where

$\overline{P}_i$ = weighted monthly proportion of interviewed groups that were AT LERs for month i for site-type HF

N_{Li} = the total number of site days in month i for stratum HF–L

N_{Mi} = the total number of site days in month i for stratum HF–M

N_{Hi} = the total number of site days in month i for stratum HF–H

$\overline{P}_L$ = proportion of interviewed groups that were AT LERs for stratum HF–L

$\overline{P}_M$ = proportion of interviewed groups that were AT LERs for stratum HF–M

$\overline{P}_H$ = proportion of interviewed groups that were AT recreationists for stratum HF–H

$\hat{V}(\overline{P}_L), \hat{V}(\overline{P}_M)$ and $\hat{V}(\overline{P}_H)$ = the estimated variances of $\overline{P}_L$, $\overline{P}_M$, and $\overline{P}_H$, respectively

The N_{Li}, N_{Mi}, and N_{Hi} are referred to as strata weights and were obtained from the prework spreadsheets. The $\overline{P}_L$, $\overline{P}_M$, $\overline{P}_H$, and their variances were estimated from the pilot study survey data from only June 1 through August 14, 2007.

To convert the NPS people tally to group tally a similar weighted mean of all group size was computed as

$$\overline{G}_i^a = \frac{N_{Li}\overline{G}_L^a \quad N_{Mi}\overline{G}_M^a \quad N_{Hi}\overline{G}_H^a}{N_{Li} \quad N_{Mi} \quad N_{Hi}} \quad (32)$$

$$\hat{V}\left(\overline{G}_i^a\right) = \frac{N_{Li}^2\hat{V}\left(\overline{G}_L^a\right) \quad N_{Mi}^2\hat{V}\left(\overline{G}_M^a\right) \quad N_{Hi}^2\hat{V}\left(\overline{G}_H^a\right)}{\left(N_{Li} \quad N_{Mi} \quad N_{Hi}\right)^2} \quad (33)$$

where

$\overline{G}_i^a$ = average size of all groups for month i for site-type HF

N_{Li} = the total number of site days in month i for stratum HF–L

N_{Mi} = the total number of site days in month i for stratum HF–M

N_{Hi} = the total number of site days in month i for stratum HF–H

$\overline{G_L^a}$ = average group size of all interviewed groups for stratum HF–L

$\overline{G_M^a}$ = average group size of all interviewed groups for stratum HF–M

$\overline{G_H^a}$ = average group size of all interviewed groups for stratum HF–H

$\hat{V}(\overline{G_L^a})$, $\hat{V}(\overline{G_M^a})$, and $\hat{V}(\overline{G_H^a})$ = the estimated variances of $\overline{G_L^a}$, $\overline{G_M^a}$, and $\overline{G_H^a}$ respectively

Also required was the monthly average group size for AT LERs defined as

$$\overline{G_i} = \frac{N_{Li}\overline{G_L} + N_{Mi}\overline{G_M} + N_{Hi}\overline{G_H}}{N_{Li} + N_{Mi} + N_{Hi}} \quad (34)$$

$$V\left(\overline{G_i}\right) = \frac{N_{Li}^2\hat{V}\left(\overline{G_L}\right) + N_{Mi}^2\hat{V}\left(\overline{G_M}\right) + N_{Hi}^2\hat{V}\left(\overline{G_H}\right)}{\left(N_{Li} + N_{Mi} + N_{Hi}\right)^2} \quad (35)$$

where

$\overline{G_i}$ = average size of all groups for month i for site-type HF

N_{Li} = the total number of site days in month i for stratum HF–L

N_{Mi} = the total number of site days in month i for stratum HF–M

N_{Hi} = the total number of site days in month i for stratum HF–H

$\overline{G_L}$ = average group size of AT LER interviewed groups for stratum HF–L

$\overline{G_M}$ = average group size of AT LER interviewed groups for stratum HF–M

$\overline{G_H}$ = average group size of AT LER interviewed groups for stratum HF–H

$\hat{V}(\overline{G_L})$, $\hat{V}(\overline{G_M})$, and $\hat{V}(\overline{G_H})$ = the estimated variances of $\overline{G_L}$, $\overline{G_M}$, and $\overline{G_H}$ respectively

The visitation for the pilot survey utilizes these monthly weighted estimates and the monthly NPS augmented site-type visitation estimate and is defined as

$$AS^S = \sum_{i=6}^{8} k\overline{P_i}\frac{AS_i^S}{\overline{G_i^a}}\overline{G_i} \quad (36)$$

where

$k = 1$ if $i = 6$ or 7 (June or July) and $k = 14/31$ if $i = 8$ (August)

AS^S = the augmented site-type visitation estimate for the pilot survey for site-type HF

AS_i^S = the official NPS visitation at Harpers Ferry, WV, for month i, $i = 6, 7, 8$

Note that in the above equation month 8 is multiplied by (14/31) to reflect that the pilot survey terminated on August 14. Also, the variance assumes that the augmented site-type visitation AS_i^S is known without error, that is, has zero variance.

The variance of the above estimator (36) is quite complicated because it is a product of a constant and three variables as well as a ratio of two correlated variables $\overline{G_i^a}$ and $\overline{G_i}$. To simplify matters, assume that $\overline{G_i^a}$ is a constant, which is reasonable because its variance is quite small. Then we have approximately

$$\hat{V}\left(AS^S\right) = \sum_{i=6}^{8} k^2\left(\frac{AS_i^S}{\overline{G_i^a}}\right)^2\left\{\overline{P_i}^2\hat{V}\left(\overline{G_i}\right) + \overline{G_i}^2\hat{V}\left(\overline{P_i}\right) - \hat{V}\left(\overline{P_i}\right)\hat{V}\left(\overline{G_i}\right)\right\} \quad (37)$$

because $\hat{V}\left(\dfrac{AS_i^S}{\overline{G_i^a}}\right) = 0$ by assumption which drops four

terms out of the general variance equation (12), simplifying the variance to a product of only two variables and two constants.

Special event—The pilot survey identified Foundry Day at Boiling Springs, PA, on June 2, 2007, as the only special event on the pilot study portion of the AT. Foundry Day was chosen as a special event day because the celebration was known to draw thousands of visitors to Boiling Springs, potentially increasing use on the AT on that day to a level greatly exceeding the defined strata. In addition, Boiling Springs consisted of a complex of five sites (998, 999, 1000, 1001, and 1002) that intersected the town, resulting in unique sampling problems. Thus, due to these issues, it was felt that these site days did not fit the criteria of any of the 13 strata and, thus, it was identified as a special event.

The methodology to estimate visitation at this special event followed the general concepts used for the other sites but with some modification. The special event estimator is the total number of AT recreation visitors in Boiling Springs, PA, on June 2, 2007, and is defined as

$$\hat{SE} = \overline{P_{SE}} \; \hat{NG}_{SE} \; \overline{G}_{SE} \tag{38}$$

with estimated variance

$$\begin{aligned}
\hat{V}\left(\hat{SE}\right) &= \overline{P_{SE}}^{2} \; \hat{NG}_{SE}^{2} \; \hat{V}\left(\overline{G_{SE}}\right) + \overline{P_{SE}}^{2} \; \overline{G_{SE}}^{2} \\
&\quad \hat{V}\left(\hat{NG}_{SE}\right) + \hat{NG}_{SE}^{2} \; \overline{G_{SE}}^{2} \; \hat{V}\left(\overline{P_{SE}}\right) \\
&\quad - \overline{P_{SE}}^{2} \hat{V}\left(\hat{NG}_{SE}\right)\hat{V}\left(\overline{G_{SE}}\right) - \hat{NG}_{SE}^{2} \; \hat{V}\left(\overline{P_{SE}}\right)\hat{V}\left(\overline{G_{SE}}\right) \\
&\quad - \overline{G_{SE}}^{2}\hat{V}\left(\overline{P_{SE}}\right)\hat{V}\left(\hat{NG}_{SE}\right) + \hat{V}\left(\overline{P_{SE}}\right)\hat{V}\left(\hat{NG}_{SE}\right)\hat{V}\left(\overline{G_{SE}}\right)
\end{aligned} \tag{39}$$

where

$\hat{SE}$ = estimator for the total number of AT recreating visitors in Boiling Springs, PA, on June 2, 2007

$\overline{P_{SE}}$ = the proportion of all groups interviewed that are AT recreating groups

$\hat{NG}_{SE}$ = the number of groups of visitors (AT and non-AT) in Boiling Springs, PA

$\overline{G}_{SE}$ = the average group size for AT recreating groups

Note that this approach deviates from the general methodology in that exiting people and vehicles are not used in the estimation process, and $\overline{P_{SE}}$ and $\overline{G}_{SE}$ were not based on the last-exiting criterion. These deviations were necessary due to the complex nature of the trail intersections in Boiling Springs.

The major difficulty was to obtain an estimate of $\hat{NG}_{SE}$, the number of groups in Boiling Springs on Foundry Day. Initial investigation indicated that many visitors came to Boiling Springs via shuttle buses operating out of a local high school. Although these groups represented a portion of $\hat{NG}_{SE}$, there were other groups that came in private

vehicles or simply walked to town. However, if somehow those who used the shuttle buses could be identified during the interviewing process, then typical mark-recapture methods used for estimating animal abundance (Seber 1982) could be used to estimate $\hat{NG}_{SE}$. This was accomplished by simply adding a question during the interview that asked if they used the shuttle buses.

The Lincoln-Petersen estimator is a simple mark-recapture estimator used for wildlife population size estimation. It consists of a two-sample process where animals are captured and marked in sample 1, and then a second sample is taken. The estimator is defined as

$$\hat{N} = \frac{(n_1 + 1)(n_2 + 1)}{(m_2 + 1)} - 1 \tag{40}$$

with estimated variance

$$\hat{V}\left(\hat{N}\right) = \frac{(n_1 + 1)(n_2 + 1)(n_1 - m_2)(n_2 - m_2)}{(m_2 + 1)^2 (m_2 + 2)} \tag{41}$$

where

$\hat{N}$ = the Lincoln-Petersen estimate of population size

n_1 = number of animals marked in first sample

n_2 = number of animals marked in second sample

m_2 = number of animals recaptured in the second sample that were marked in the first sample

Applying the Lincoln-Peterson estimator to Boiling Springs, PA, let the first sample be the groups that took the shuttle bus and the second sample be the groups interviewed in town during the interviewing process. Although the groups in the first sample were not physically "marked," they could be detected in sample 2 by asking the additional question "Did you take the shuttle bus to town?" Thus, for this application,

NG = number of visiting groups in Boiling Springs, PA

n_1 = number of groups that took the shuttle bus

n_2 = number of groups interviewed in Boiling Springs, PA

m_2 = number of groups interviewed that took the shuttle bus

Although the shuttle bus count was based on people, it may be converted to groups to give

$$n = \frac{C^b}{\overline{G^b}} \qquad (42)$$

where

C^b = the total number of people that took the shuttle bus

$\overline{G^b}$ = the average group size for those groups that took the shuttle bus

An estimator $\hat{NG}$ for the number of groups in Boiling Springs, PA, is obtained by substituting these quantities into the general Lincoln-Petersen estimator [equation (40)].

One component of the survey process at Boiling Springs, PA, consisted of shuttle bus tallies. The shuttle bus operated from 9:00 a.m. to 4:00 p.m. and transported people from the high school to the festivities in town. Survey personnel stationed at the school tallied 610 people being transported to town (table 4). However, the observer took a break between 10:59 a.m. and 11:50 a.m. (51 minutes) and, thus, the tally does not include this interval. To estimate the number of people on the buses during the break, the average number of people per minute was determined for approximately an hour before and an hour after the break. The hour before the break included the 10:02 to immediately prior 10:59 (57 minutes) bus tallies, totaling 191 people. The hour after the break included the 11:50 a.m. to immediately prior 12:50 p.m. (60 minutes) bus tallies, totaling 94 people. The average people per minute is, thus, calculated as $(191+94) / (57+60)$ = 2.44. The break was 51 minutes so the number of people during this interval is $51(2.44) = 124$. Note that although the break with no tallies was 51 minutes, the interval used was defined to include the 10:59 a.m. to immediately prior to the 11:50 a.m. bus tally which totaled 33 people. This is analogous to the methodology previously used to obtain the hourly bus tallies. Thus, subtracting the number taken on the bus at the beginning of the break (10:59) from 124 gives the total number of unseen break bus people as $124-33 = 91$. The total number of bus people is the sum of those seen on the buses plus those unseen people during the break, yielding $C^b = 610 + 91 = 701$.

The other survey component was the interviewing process. This was performed at two of the five sites (999 and 1000) in Boiling Springs from 8:00 a.m. to 4:00 p.m. following the standard procedure with the addition of the extra question pertaining to the shuttle bus. A total of 26 groups were interviewed—with 12 using the AT for recreation, 10 not using the AT for recreation, and 4 refusing to answer the interview. Thus, the proportion of groups that used the AT for recreation was $\overline{P_{SE}} = 12 / 22 = 0.5455$ with $\hat{V}(\overline{P_{SE}}) = 0.0113$ and $n_2 = 22$. During this period there

were $m_2 = 2$ groups interviewed that took the shuttle bus with their average group size being $\overline{G^b} = 3.0$ and, thus, using equation (42) $n_1 = 701 / 3.0 = 233.67$. For simplicity, ignore the variance and assume that n_1 is a constant. In addition, there were 11 groups interviewed that used the AT for recreation and for which group sizes were obtained, yielding an average group size of $\overline{G_{SE}} = 3.0909$ with variance $\hat{V}(\overline{G_{SE}}) = 0.5901$.

Table 4—The Boiling Springs, PA, shuttle bus tallies on June 2, 2007

Departure time	Shuttle bus people count	Return time
	number	
9:00	35	9:08
9:11	20	9:19
9:20	25	9:27
9:25	14	9:32
9:33	21	9:42
9:41	33	9:49
9:48	23	9:57
10:02	48	10:11
10:10	32	10:20
10:19	25	10:28
10:29	42	10:40
10:38	10	10:46
10:49	34	11:01
10:59	33	—
—	91 [a]	—
11:50	35	12:03
12:02	24	12:13
12:12	20	12:23
12:20	8	12:29
12:28	3	12:39
12:35	4	12:44
12:50	11	1:01
1:03	25	1:14
1:10	20	1:20
1:21	4	1:30
1:25	8	1:34
1:36	8	1:46
1:40	5	1:48
1:51	10	2:00
2:08	7	2:19
2:14	5	2:24
2:25	1	2:33
2:32	2	2:38
2:40	1	2:47
2:48	0	2:58
2:53	2	3:03
3:04	5	3:13
3:14	1	3:22
3:23	0	3:34
3:28	6	3:52
4:01	0	4:10

— = no observations taken.

[a] A break was taken between 10:59 and 11:50 so no observations were recorded for the shuttle buses leaving between this interval. The value here is an approximation which is derived in the text.

The above estimates could be used to obtain an estimate for $\hat{SE}$. Using the general Lincoln-Petersen estimator [equation (40)]

$$\hat{NG} = \frac{(233.67+1)(22+1)}{(2+1)} - 1 = 1798$$

with estimated variance [equation (41)]

$$\hat{V}\left(\hat{NG}\right) =$$

$$\frac{(233.67+1)(22+1)(233.67-2)(22-2)}{(2+1)^2(2+2)} = 694{,}677$$

and substituting values into equation (38) yields the special event estimate

$$\hat{SE} = 0.5455(1798)(3.0909) = 3{,}032$$

with estimated variance [equation (39)] $\hat{V}\left(\hat{SE}\right) = 3{,}114{,}724$

Databases and Computer Programs

There are several types of data files created or collected in the pilot survey that have been archived as Microsoft Excel® files (table 5). These consist of prework spreadsheet files and the sample calendar and sample backup file created from them. In addition, the observed data collected during the sample days are in the day summary and individual interview files. The augmented site data from the NPS are in two other files. Each of these will now be briefly discussed.

The initial step in the pilot survey was to create the sampling frame from which the sample was eventually selected. To accomplish this, all exiting sites in the pilot region had to be identified. In addition, to perform an extrapolation to the entire AT, all sites had to be identified on the entire AT. This consisted of six prework spreadsheet files. The procedure for data entry follows that explained previously in the prework dataset section. The variable names, type, length, description, and permissible values are shown in table 6. The sample calendar and sample backup days were generated via a SAS program (SAS Institute Inc. 2004) that randomly selected the sample days according to specified criteria (table 5).

Table 5—Data files and SAS programs used in the pilot survey and trailwide extrapolation to the entire AT

File name	Description	Records[a]
		number
PilotRegion_10152008_SZ.xls	Prework	409
ATCHRegion_10282008_SZ.xls	Prework	11
NewEnglandRegion_10142008_LLSZ.xls	Prework	631
MidAtlanticRegion_10202008_LLSZ.xls	Prework	770
Virginia_10142008_LLSZ.xls	Prework	467
SouthernRegion_10142008_LLSZ.xls	Prework	348
calendar.xls	Sample calendar	141
backup.xls	Sample backup sample days	184
ATCH_calendar.xls	ATC sample calendar	6
DSF_A_082008.xls	Original day summary data	133
DSF_B_082108_SZMB.xls	Slightly edited day summary data	130
DSF_C_100908_SZMB.xls	Final day summary data	130
IND_A_082008.xls	Original individual interview data	1,432
IND_B_082108_SZMB.xls	Slightly edited individual interview data	1,414
IND_C_090308_SZMB.xls	Final individual interview data	1,233
ATCPROXY_101508_SZ.xls	ATC augmented visit data	365
HFPROXY_10092008_SZ.xls	Harpers Ferry augmented visit data	12
Prework_04252007.sas	SAS program to generate the sampling calendar	398
Prework_ATC.sas	SAS program to generate the sampling calendar for the ATC	46
estimation_02252009.sas	SAS program to produce the estimates	3,310

AT = Appalachian National Scenic Trail; ATC = Appalachian Trail Conservancy.
[a] Does not include the header record if the file is a Microsoft Excel® (.xls) data file.

The observed data consist of standard and augmented site data. The day summary files contain basic information about the interviewer and the interview process for each sample day. Three levels of files are archived. The first level is A, which consists of data as entered from the field with no edit corrections. This file has limited applications but serves as a benchmark for the original data. Level B consists of the data after minor, obvious errors have been corrected with what are known to be true corrections. These data may be useful to certain investigators wanting to analyze the data recording process itself or perform edit corrections based on their own decisions. Level C is a further modification where questionable data were altered based on certain logical considerations and knowledge about the survey process. These are the data that were considered the best for all estimates for the pilot survey. Information about the variables and their characteristics is listed in table 7. The individual interview files are the data recorded for each group interviewed for all the sample days. There are the A, B, and C versions that serve the same purposes as outlined for the day summary files. Table 8 gives the characteristics for the variables. The augmented

site data are in two files, one for the site-type ATCH (ATCPROXY_101508_SZ.xls) and the other for the site-type HF (HFPROXY_10092008.xls).

All mathematical and statistical computations were performed with SAS-generated programs (SAS Institute Inc. 2004). A consistent, structured style was used in the programming process, and numerous comments were incorporated to aid in explanation of the programming steps. The prework programs were developed to read in the prework spreadsheets, develop the sampling frame, and then select the sample days according to the sample design. Two programs performed this function, one for the ATC and another for the rest of the pilot region. The major programming effort was to develop the SAS estimation program which produced the many estimated parameters and eventual visitation estimates based on the stratified random cluster sampling design. These SAS programs are listed in table 5.

Table 6—The prework data file showing variable names, type, length, description, and permissible values

Variable	Type	Length	Description	Values[a]
SITENUM	N	8	Site number	0 to 1015
SITETYPE	C	3	Site-type	ATC, M[b], P, S[c], TR
USELEVEL	C	1	Use-level	L, M, H
BEGIN	N	8	Beginning date span	101 to 1225
END	N	8	Ending date span	101 to 1231
MONDAY	N	8	1 = day has this use-level Blank = does not have this use-level	1, blank
TUESDAY	N	8	1 = day has this use-level Blank = does not have this use-level	1, blank
WEDNESDAY	N	8	1 = day has this use-level Blank = does not have this use-level	1, blank
THURSDAY	N	8	1 = day has this use-level Blank = does not have this use-level	1, blank
FRIDAY	N	8	1 = day has this use-level Blank = does not have this use-level	1, blank
SATURDAY	N	8	1 = day has this use-level Blank = does not have this use-level	1, blank
SUNDAY	N	8	1 = day has this use-level Blank = does not have this use-level	1, blank
HOLIDAY	N	8	1 = day has this use-level Blank = does not have this use-level	1, blank

N = numeric variable; C = character variable; ATC = Appalachian Trail Conservancy; TR = trail/road; L = low; M = medium; H = high.
[a] All character values are case sensitive.
[b] The site-type MU is coded as M in the data.
[c] The site-type HF is coded as S in the data.

Pilot Survey Results

Parameter estimates—The calibrating parameters consist of the $\overline{P}_h$, $\overline{G}_h$, and $\overline{G}_h^a$ which were estimated with the design-based and model-based approaches. A comparison of these reveals that the model-based approach produces more stable and plausible estimates for the limited amount of data available from the pilot survey. The estimated $\overline{P}_h$ and standard errors for all strata for both approaches are shown in table 9. The design-based approach yields for site-type TR an estimated $\overline{P}_h$ = 0.500 for use-level L and $\overline{P}_h$ = 1.000 for use-level M. Recalling that $\overline{P}_h$ is the proportion of exiting groups that are recreating and not returning to the AT on that day, it seems unreasonable that the true parameter values are so incongruent. This is probably due to the extremely low sample size of only eight and two interviewed groups, respectively. A similar problem occurs for stratum HF–L when compared to strata HF–M and HF–H. Alternately, the model-based approach produces more plausible parameter estimates in these situations because it incorporates the data from all site-types and use-levels to produce much smoother relationships as shown in figure 6. For all site-types, use-level L is substantially less than M and H which are practically identical. In addition, the highest $\overline{P}_h$ is for site-type P followed by TR. This should be expected because these site-types are typically used only by AT hikers. The ATCH site-type is intermediate due to an approximate mixture of AT and non-AT visitors. Site-type MU, e.g., State parks through which the AT runs, is a little lower, reflecting higher percentages of non-AT visitors. The lowest $\overline{P}_h$ is for site-type HF due to the large proportion of visitors that are recreating at Harpers Ferry National Historical Park and not using the AT. The standard errors are also more reasonable for the model-based approach. They are much smoother and are usually less than half that of the design-based approach. The estimated $\overline{G}_h$ and $\overline{G}_h^a$ reveal similar trends, being smoother and more realistic for the model-based approach (tables 10 and 11) (figs. 7 and 8). Although the standard errors are usually lower for the model-based approach, they are not as substantially so as was the case for $\overline{P}_h$. It is also interesting to note that the model-based estimate for $\overline{G}_h^a$ is approximately 18 percent larger than that of $\overline{G}_h$. This supports the need for incorporating both $\overline{G}_h^a$ and $\overline{G}_h$ in the visitation estimators as was given in the "Estimation Methodology" section of Part I.

The results for the pilot survey parameter estimates reveal several justifications for preferring the model-based approach over the design-based approach. First, limited available resources resulted in low-sampling intensity for certain strata which increased the risk of erratic estimates for the design-based approach. This was alleviated to a certain extent with the model-based approach because all the data are pooled, the relationship between site-type and use-level are modeled, and then the individual strata estimates are obtained from the model. Second, the model-based approach smoothes out the parameter estimates so that inconsistencies are eliminated to a large degree. For instance, if a parameter increases with increasing use-level for a given site-type, it will exhibit this pattern for the other site-types. The design-based approach does not have this property because the individual strata estimates are

Table 7—The day summary data file consists of 17 variables and 130 observations (the variables are currently in the file in this order based on the questionnaire, although a reordering may be more appropriate for clarity)

Variable	Type	Length	Description	Values[a]
VEHICLESTART	N	8	Number of vehicles in parking lot at start of interview period	0 to 89
START	N	8	Time at start of interview period (military)	800 to 1630
INTERVIEWER	C	14	Person conducting interviews	Any name
CLICKPERSON	C	14	Person using clicker	Any name
DATE	N	8	Date of the survey	6/1/2007 to 8/14/2007
SITENUM	N	8	Site number	0 to 1015
SITENAME	C	27	Site name	Any name
WEATHER	C	19	Weather conditions	Any text
BREAK	N	8	Break time (minutes)	0 to 90
END	N	8	Time at end of interview period (military)	1300 to 2010
SUBSTITUTE	C	5	Is this a substitute day?	NO, YES, EXTRA
ORIGINAL	C	17	Original SITENUM and day if a substitute day	Any text
CLICKER	N	8	Total clicker count at end of interview period	0 to 230
TYPE	C	8	What was counted[b]	HIKERS, VEHICLES, NOTHING
VEHICLEEND	N	8	Number of vehicles in parking lot at end of interview period	0 to 150
SURVEYS	N	8	Total number of all surveys completed at end of interview period	0 to 58
NOTES	C	502	Notes	Any text

N = numeric variable; C = character variable.

[a] All character values are case sensitive.

[b] Vehicles were counted at sites 825, 828, 840, 841, 878, 919, 955, and 999. Site 810, 811, and 813 are blank because there was no counting done. Hikers were counted at all other sites.

Table 8—The individual interview data file consists of 43 variables and 1,233 observations (180 were RETURN which were deleted) (the variables are currently in the file in this order based on the questionnaire, although a reordering may be more appropriate for clarity)

Variable	Type	Length	Description	Values[a]
INTERVIEWER	C	15	Person conducting interviews	Any name
MONTH	N	8	Month for the survey	6, 7, 8
DAY	N	8	Day of the survey	1 to 30
YEAR	N	8	Year of the survey	2007
SITENUM	N	8	Site number	0 to 1015
SITETYPE	C	3	Site-type	ATC, M[b], P, S[c], TR
SITENAME	C	27	Site name	Any name
AGREE	N	8	Person agreed to take survey 0 = no 1 = yes	0, 1
MATHER	N	8	0 = no (only at ATC) 1 = yes	0, 1
ATUSE	N	8	Person used the AT today 0 = no 1 = yes	0, 1
REASON	C	9	Is AT the primary or secondary reason for the visit?	PRIMARY, SECONDARY
PURPOSE	N	8	Purpose of visit 1 = recreation 2 = nonrecreation	1, 2
EXIT	C	5	Leaving AT for the day	LEAVE
TRANS	C	7	Transportation mode to AT	VEHICLE, BUS, BICYCLE, WALKING, OTHER
ARRMONTH	N	8	Month arrived at AT	2, 3, 4, 5, 6, 7, 8
ARRDAY	N	8	Day arrived at AT	1 to 30
ARRYEAR	N	8	Year arrived at AT	2007
ARRTIME	N	8	Time arrived at AT (military)	500 to 2130
HIKE	N	8	Hiking distance on AT today 1 = < or = 1 mile 2 = over 1 but < 5 miles 3 = 5 to < 10 miles 4 = 10 or more miles	1, 2, 3, 4
VISITS	N	8	Visits to this AT site in last 12 months[d]	0 to 364
ATVISITS	N	8	Visits to any AT site in last 12 months[d]	0 to 365
ATVISITS_ADJ	N	8	Adjusted visits to any AT site in last 12 months[d] (corrects original data errors)[e]	0 to 365
MALES	N	8	Males in group	0 to 22
FEMALES	N	8	Females in group	0 to 21
MALES16	N	8	Males < 16 in group	0 to 12
FEMALES16	N	8	Females < 16 in group	0 to 10
NIGHTS	N	8	Continuous nights on AT before today	0 to 100
SATISFIED	N	8	Satisfaction with AT 1 = least satisfied 10 = most satisfied	5, 6, 7, 8, 9, 10
CROWDED	N	8	Crowding on AT 1 = not at all crowded 9 = extremely crowded	1, 2, 3, 4, 5, 6, 7, 8, 9
MANAGE	C	82	Management Improvements	Any text
SPEND	N	8	Spent for this AT visit (dollars)	0 to 8000
ZIPCODE	N	8	Zip code	1945 to 99999

continued

Table 8—The individual interview data file consists of 43 variables and 1,233 observations (180 were RETURN which were deleted) (the variables are currently in the file in this order based on the questionnaire, although a reordering may be more appropriate for clarity) (continued)

Variable	Type	Length	Description	Values[a]
AGE	N	8	Age class	16, 21, 31, 41, 51, 61, 71
			16 = 16 to 20	
			21 = 21 to 30	
			31 = 31 to 40	
			41 = 41 to 50	
			51 = 51 to 60	
			61 = 61 to 70	
			71 = 71+	
GENDER	C	1	Gender	F, M
HISPANIC	N	8	Hispanic or Latino	0, 1
NATIVE	N	8	American Indian/Alaska Native	0, 1
ASIAN	N	8	Asian	0, 0, 11
BLACK	N	8	Black	0,1
PACIFIC	N	8	Native Hawaiian/Pacific Islander	0, 1
WHITE	N	8	White	0, 1
REFUSED	N	8	Refused racial questions	0, 1
CLICKER	N	8	Clicker count including this interview	0 to 229
TIME	N	8	Time at interview end (military)	802 to 1957

C = character variable; N = numeric variable; ATC = Appalachian Trail Conservancy ; M = multiple use; P = parking; S = Harpers Ferry; TR = trail/road; AT = Appalachian National Scenic Trail; F = female; M = male.

[a] All character values are case sensitive.

[b] The site-type MU is coded as M in the data.

[c] The site-type HF is coded as S in the data.

[d] Does not include this visit.

[e] Equals ATVISITS if VISITS is less than or equal to ATVISITS but equals VISITS+ATVISITS if VISITS greater than ATVISITS.

not linked via a common model. Third, the standard errors of the parameter estimates are substantially smaller with the model-based approach because all the data are pooled and used jointly in the estimation process for all strata estimates of a parameter. Alternatively, the design-based approach estimates a stratum's parameter based only on the data observed in that stratum which results in a smaller sample size and, consequently, a larger standard error.

Despite the advantages of the model-based approach when the sampling intensity is low, the design-based approach is preferred when adequate sampling is affordable and has been achieved. In this situation, the sample-based estimate for a given stratum is independent of the other strata and is capable of reflecting its individual characteristics and properties. It does not rely on a model which assumes no interaction between site-type and use-level. This may be unrealistic in some surveys.

Guidelines for when to use the two estimation approaches are based on professional judgment and somewhat arbitrary rules of thumb. Generally, the goal in a survey is to estimate a parameter with a coefficient of variation (CV) of 10 percent or less. The CV is the ratio of the standard error divided by the parameter estimate converted to a percent. To achieve this for a proportion such as $\overline{P}_h$ under simple random sampling requires a sample size of 100 when the estimate of $\overline{P}_h$ is 0.5. The pilot survey was a cluster design so the calculation of required sample size is more complicated because sample size is defined by primary (clusters) and secondary (total number of observations within the clusters) sampling units. However, it is generally accepted that clustering is less efficient than simple random sampling, so it is safe to assume that the sample size of the secondary sampling units should be over 100. Referring to table 9, this criterion is not met for most of the strata. When parameter estimates are based on means such as $\overline{G}_h$ and $\overline{G}_h^a$, the calculation of required sample size is different, but generally a sample size of 30 is considered minimal for simple random sampling. Tables 10 and 11 reveal that the number of secondary sampling units is usually < 30 which is inadequate, even if one discards the cluster nature of the sampling design.

Another factor to consider when comparing the design-based and model-based approaches is subject matter expertise. Usually an analyst will have some knowledge about the parameters that are being estimated and can judge which approach produces more desirable estimates. For instance, the design-based approach yielded $\overline{P}_h$ = 0.500 for the TR–L stratum and $\overline{P}_h$ = 1.000 for the TR–M stratum (table 9). It seems highly unlikely that there would be such a difference in $\overline{P}_h$ between the L and M use-levels within the site-type TR. The model-based approach yields estimates of $\overline{P}_h$ = 0.586 for the TR–L stratum and $\overline{P}_h$ = 0.695 for the TR–H stratum (table 9) which appear to be more plausible. Thus, if this occurs for several of the strata, the model-based approach is the more desirable approach. However,

Table 9—The estimated $\overline{P}_h$ for each site-type and use-level using the design-based approach and the model-based approach

Site-type	Use-level	Clusters	n	Design-based $\overline{P}_h$	Design-based SE	Model-based $\overline{P}_h$	Model-based SE
		number					
TR	L	6	8	0.500	0.256	0.586	0.124
TR	M	2	2	1.000	0.000	0.655	0.130
TR	H	0	0	1.000[a]	0.000[a]	0.695	0.130
P	L	5	9	0.650	0.138	0.696	0.053
P	M	10	40	0.696	0.221	0.765	0.036
P	H	18	205	0.819	0.115	0.805	0.025
MU	L	4	33	0.273	0.123	0.204	0.049
MU	M	13	92	0.273	0.104	0.273	0.031
MU	H	20	196	0.300	0.087	0.313	0.025
HF	L	2	56	0.018	0.022	0.061	0.049
HF	M	4	85	0.165	0.061	0.129	0.030
HF	H	10	341	0.164	0.037	0.170	0.020
ATCH	L	0	0	0.278[b]	0.130[b]	0.355	0.079
ATCH	M	2	18	0.278	0.130	0.424	0.067
ATCH	H	4	59	0.508	0.124	0.464	0.063

SE = standard error; TR = trail/road; P = parking; MU = multiple use; HF = Harpers Ferry; ATCH = Appalachian Trail Conservancy Headquarters; L= low; M = medium;H = high.

[a] The TR–H stratum had no sample days so the design-based approach $\overline{P}_h$ and SE are based on the TR–M stratum.

[b] The ATCH–L stratum had no sample days so the design-based approach $\overline{P}_h$ and SE are based on the ATCH–M stratum.

caution must be used here to avoid selecting the approach that simply yields parameter estimates that result in any preconceived estimate of visitation that the analyst wishes to attain from the survey data.

The average daily clicker count for each strata was computed for the standard site-types TR, P, and MU as explained previously. They represent the average number of people based on a 12-hour day for all groups whether they represent LERs or not. The results follow what was anticipated with site-type TR being the lowest, site-type P being intermediate, and site-type MU being the largest (table 12). The use-level relationship was also logical, with L being less than M which was less than H. This is not only reassuring here but also provides further evidence that the prework and stratification process were valid.

The ATCH daily augmented site tallies obtained from the ATCH ranged from 10 to 191 during the pilot survey period (table 13). Recall that these are the total number of people that exited the ATCH during a given day. The daily average for the two use-levels was 38.50 for M and 70.59 for H, which intuitively reflects the prework classification and stratification. The conversion from number of people

to number of groups (LER and non-LER) resulted in 14.78 for M and 27.31 for H.

The 2007 augmented site data for the site-type HF strata were obtained from the official NPS Harpers Ferry National Historical Park visitation estimates and reflects the sites 810, 811, and 813 (National Park Service 2008). The NPS monthly values ranged from 2,447 in February to 40,522 in July. In order to obtain estimates as outlined in the "Estimation Methodology" section of Part I, monthly weights had to be obtained for the three use-levels from which monthly weighted estimates of $\overline{P}_i$, $\overline{G}_i$, and $\overline{G}_i^a$ were computed (table 14). There was little variation for each of these estimates over the months. The $\overline{P}_i$ ranged from 0.074 to 0.096 with standard errors from 0.0305 to 0.0400. The $\overline{G}_i$ was even more consistent and ranged from 2.47 to 2.50 with standard errors from 0.387 to 0.508. The $\overline{G}_i^a$ were also quite consistent and ranged from 2.81 to 2.85 with standard errors ranging from 0.151 to 0.198.

Pilot survey visitation estimates—The visitation estimates were calculated based on the previous described methodology using the calibrating parameter estimates obtained by the design-based and model-based approaches.

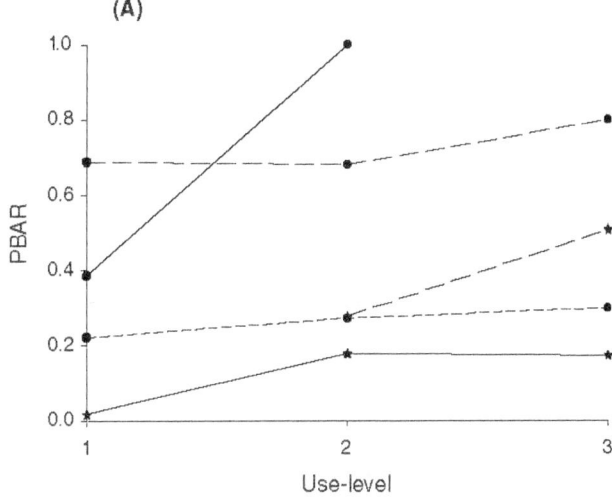

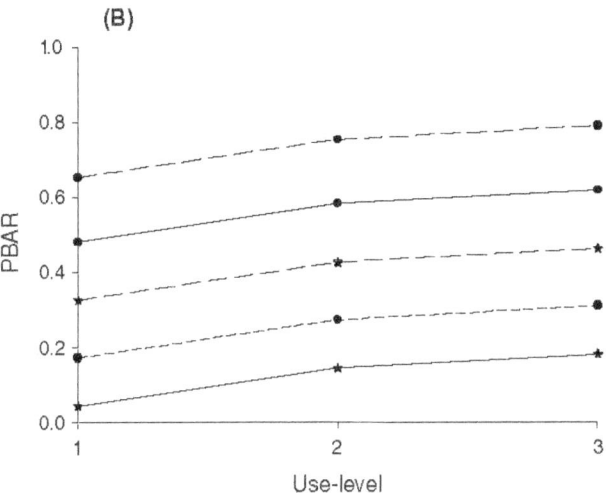

Figure 6—The relationship of estimated $\overline{P}_h$ and use-level for the five site-types using (A) the design-based approach and (B) the model-based approach. The circles represent the standard strata where TR = solid, P = long dash, and MU = short dash. The stars represent the augmented strata where HF = solid and ATCH = long dash.

The estimates based on each stratum along with standard errors, CVs, and 95-percent confidence intervals are shown in table 15. Converting total visits in each stratum to visits per day reveals the logical trends for the use-levels. Although there were many TR sites, average daily visits were slightly < 3 according to either approach. The site-types P and MU were similar in visitation over the use-levels, with L being < 10 for both, while H ranged to near 60. The augmented site ATCH average daily visitation was about 17 for M and 30 for H. The augmented site-type HF did not allow for individual use-level estimates because only monthly augmented data were available.

The pilot survey estimates reveal that the bulk of the visitation is from the P and MU site-types. Although there are many TR site days, the average visits per day are so low that their total visits are only about half or less than

those of site-types MU or P. Nevertheless, because of the large number of site days, the TR–L stratum produces the second most visits of any individual stratum (table 15). The augmented site-types ATCH and HF have relatively large average daily visitation but have few site days which also result in low total visitation.

A comparison of the total visit estimates on a strata basis for the two approaches reveals that they are quite similar for site-type P, MU, and ATCH for use-level H while for the other two use-levels they were substantially different with no pattern being exhibited. The estimates for site-type TR varied depending on use-level with the model-based approach being lower for use-level L while the design-based approach was lower for use-level M. The ATCH site-type produced very nearly the same estimates for both approaches, but the HF site-type was much different with the model-based approach yielding almost three times as much visitation as the design-based approach. The precision of the estimates which depends on the standard error is best viewed through the CV which gives the standard error as a percent of the estimates. In nearly all strata the CV for the model-based approach is less than the design-based approach. Despite this, both approaches have CVs that are usually much over 15 percent. This is reflected in many of the confidence intervals being very wide, with some actually having negative values. Thus, strata-level estimates of visitation should be viewed with caution because of the large level of variability due to small sample size. It should be remembered that the objective of this survey was for an overall estimate in the pilot area and not strata-level estimates. If strata-level estimates are needed for future surveys, the sample sizes should be increased accordingly.

The comparison of the design-based and model-based approaches indicates that very different estimates may often be obtained due to the differences in estimating the calibration parameters $\overline{P}_h$, $\overline{G}_h$, and $\overline{G}_h^a$ as described previously. In this case, the model-based approach appears more consistent with logical relationships for these calibration parameters than the design-based approach. In addition, it produces smaller estimates of the standard errors of the calibration parameters and strata visitation estimates. Thus, the pilot survey visitation estimate will be based upon the model-based approach. However, in other surveys it is recommended that the design-based approach be considered, especially when sufficient sample size is available to produce more stable estimates.

The pilot survey was principally designed to obtain overall visitation from June 1 through August 14, 2007, on the AT from Harpers Ferry, WV, to 10 trail miles north of Boiling Springs, PA, at the Scott Farm. Thus, combining the model-based estimates over the standard site-types, the augmented site-type ATCH, the augmented site-type HF, and the special event yields the visitation estimates shown in table 16. The total visitation for the pilot survey using

Table 10—The estimated $\overline{G}_h$ for each site-type and use-level using the design-based approach and the model-based approach

Site-type	Use-level	Clusters	n	Design-based $\overline{G}_h$	Design-based SE	Model-based $\overline{G}_h$	Model-based SE
		number					
TR	L	4	4	3.000	2.126	2.377	0.893
TR	M	2	2	1.000	0.000	2.246	0.960
TR	H	0	0	1.000[a]	0.000[a]	2.385	0.963
P	L	4	6	2.375	0.861	2.699	0.579
P	M	10	25	2.748	0.910	2.567	0.297
P	H	18	174	2.690	0.150	2.706	0.159
MU	L	3	9	2.600	0.421	2.602	0.570
MU	M	9	25	2.109	0.246	2.470	0.309
MU	H	12	59	2.771	0.370	2.609	0.250
HF	L	1	1	1.000	0.000[b]	2.506	0.623
HF	M	4	14	2.571	0.823	2.374	0.346
HF	H	10	63	2.478	0.332	2.514	0.260
ATCH	L	0	0	4.000[c]	0.800[c]	2.441	0.767
ATCH	M	2	5	4.000	0.800	2.309	0.568
ATCH	H	4	30	2.167	0.343	2.449	0.511

SE = standard error; TR = trail/road; P = parking; MU = multiple use; HF = Harpers Ferry; ATCH = Appalachian Trail Conservancy Headquarters; L= low; M = medium; H = high.

[a] The TR–H stratum had no sample days so the design-based approach $\overline{G}_h$ and SE are based on the TR–M stratum.

[b] The HF–L stratum had only one observation so the design-based approach SE was set to 0.000 for computational simplicity.

[c] The ATCH–L stratum had no sample days so the design-based approach $\overline{G}_h$ and SE are based on the ATCH–M stratum.

the model-based approach was 70,912 with 95-percent confidence intervals of 48,678 to 93,146. The CV was 16 percent which is considered quite good especially for the low level of sampling that was performed. The bulk of the visitation (83 percent) could be attributed to the standard sites types. The three HF sites at Harpers Ferry contributed a moderate share (9 percent), while the ATCH had a relatively small contribution (3 percent). However, it should be noted that these augmented site-types (HF and ATCH) in Harpers Ferry account for about 12 percent of all AT visitation for the pilot survey. This is a large share considering the mileage of the AT running through Harpers Ferry relative to the mileage of the AT included in the pilot survey.

Part II—Trailwide Extrapolation (TWE)

Overview

The estimates from the pilot survey were based on data collected over the spatial and temporal inference spaces defined by the objectives of the survey; however, resource limitations precluded sampling over the entire AT for the whole year. Thus, for the TWE, some caution must be used when interpreting the various estimates and when using these estimates for management purposes. The first major assumption that was imposed is that the calibrating parameters $\overline{P}_h$, $\overline{G}_h$, and $\overline{G}_h^a$ for the TWE are the same as for the pilot survey. The stratification process of classifying site days into site-types and use-levels should theoretically help to satisfy this assumption to a certain degree. For example, if a site was in stratum MU–L during the pilot survey, its group size $\overline{G}_h$ is probably quite similar to another site in stratum MU–L during the winter. However, it must be emphasized that the spring, fall, and winter did not contribute any standard site data to the estimates and, thus, it is inevitable that some differences could exist temporally and spatially. A second major assumption that may be more critical and difficult to accept is that the exit tallies $\overline{C}_h$ are the same for the pilot survey and the TWE. Although this issue was carefully considered and incorporated into the stratification process used for the whole AT, the pilot survey strata sample means could potentially be biased upwards with respect to the TWE because they are based only on summer data when there

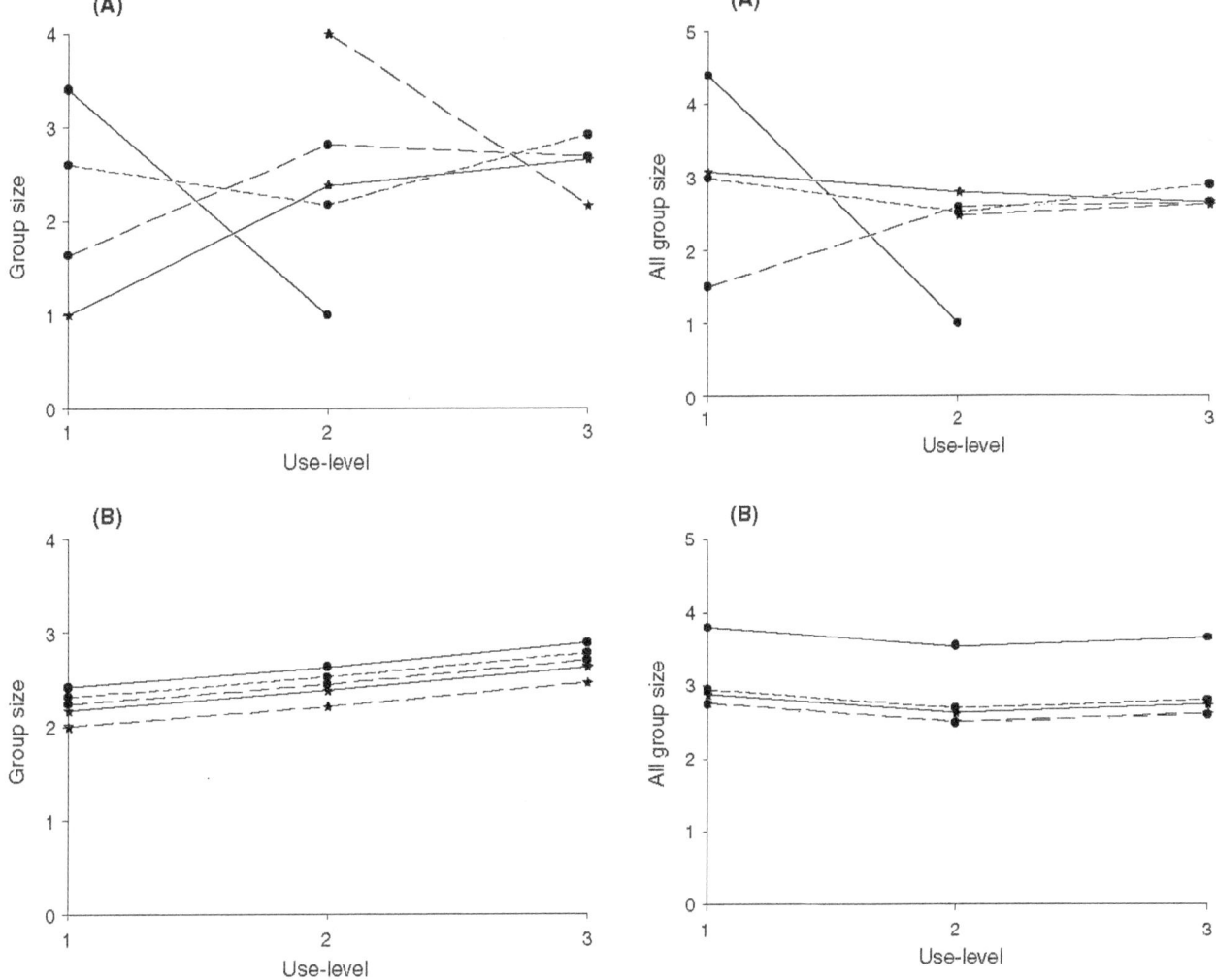

Figure 7—The relationship of estimated $\overline{G}_h$ and use-level for the five site-types using (A) the design-based approach and (B) the model-based approach. The circles represent the standard strata where TR = solid, P = long dash, and MU = short dash. The stars represent the augmented strata where HF = solid and ATCH = long dash.

Figure 8—The relationship of estimated $\overline{G}_h^a$ and use-level for the five site-types using (A) the design-based approach and (B) the model-based approach. The circles represent the standard strata where TR = solid, P = long dash, and MU = short dash. The stars represent the augmented strata where HF = solid and ATCH = long dash.

is more opportunity for larger groups with children to use the AT. A final major assumption for the TWE is that there were no festivals or events analogous to the special event at Boiling Springs where AT usage would have exceeded the L, M, and H exit volume levels for the various site-types. Omitting such days or events could lead to a negative bias in the extrapolation results. Despite these problems, the TWE estimation process described below is the optimal approach in lieu of the resources necessary to sample along the entire AT during the course of a complete year.

Sampling Design

The first step in the TWE was the prework which developed the sampling frame consisting of all site days along the entire AT from Mount Katahdin, ME, to Springer Mountain,

GA, from January 1, 2007, to December 31, 2007. This was performed as was described for the pilot survey and included the New England, mid-Atlantic, Virginia, and southern regions. Stratification was formed by the classification of all site days into the 15 potential strata formed by the combination of the 5 site-types and 3 use-levels. Unlike the pilot survey, the TWE did contain site days in strata ATCH–L and TR–H in which case special modifications were employed to obtain the intermediate quantities needed for visitation estimation. Due to limited resources and time, no other sites were added to the site-type HF strata except those previously discussed at Harpers Ferry, WV, which were expanded to include the entire year. This was also the case for site-type ATCH. Similarly, no special events other than Foundry Day at Boiling Springs, PA, on June 2 were identified for the TWE. Undoubtedly there may be other

Table 11—The estimated $\overline{G_h^a}$ for each site-type and use-level using the design-based approach and the model-based approach

Site-type	Use-level	Clusters	n	Design-based $\overline{G_h^a}$	Design-based SE	Model-based $\overline{G_h^a}$	Model-based SE
		number					
TR	L	6	8	4.500	1.944	3.838	0.631
TR	M	2	2	1.000	0.000	3.649	0.662
TR	H	0	0	1.000[a]	0.000[a]	3.630	0.661
P	L	5	9	1.800	0.508	2.817	0.263
P	M	10	40	2.561	0.649	2.629	0.177
P	H	18	204	2.664	0.110	2.610	0.129
MU	L	5	41	2.896	0.452	2.943	0.236
MU	M	13	101	2.542	0.216	2.755	0.149
MU	H	19	189	2.871	0.249	2.736	0.128
HF	L	2	54	3.074	0.348	2.887	0.242
HF	M	4	110	2.973	0.266	2.698	0.143
HF	H	10	384	2.584	0.105	2.679	0.096
ATCH	L	0	0	2.474[b]	0.061[b]	2.792	0.398
ATCH	M	2	19	2.474	0.061	2.604	0.337
ATCH	H	4	59	2.627	0.545	2.585	0.321

SE = standard error; TR = trail/road; P = parking; MU = multiple use; HF = Harpers Ferry; ATCH = Appalachian Trail Conservancy Headquarters; L= low; M = medium; H = high.

[a] The TR–H stratum had no sample days so the design-based approach $\overline{G_h^a}$ and SE are based on the TR–M stratum.

[b] The ATCH–L stratum had no sample days so the design-based approach $\overline{G_h^a}$ and SE are based on the ATCH–M stratum.

site days along the AT with extraordinary characteristics like the site-types HF and ATCH, and special event at Boiling Springs. If such site days exist and are not explicitly accounted for, the TWE will exhibit a negative bias and be conservative. Future recommendations suggest that efforts be used to identify such sites along the entire AT.

The total TWE sampling frame consisted of 332,434 site days excluding the special event distributed by site-type and use-level as shown in table 2. The TR–L stratum had the most site days, totaling 56 percent of the entire sampling frame followed by P–L with 24 percent. Although these two strata may represent low levels of daily visitation, they comprise 80 percent of all site days and, therefore, may have a large impact on the visitation estimate. The TWE designated all TR, P, and MU as standard site-types and the HF and ATCH as augmented site-types.

The number of sites identified as unique exit points for each of the regions was New England = 239, mid-Atlantic (excluding pilot) = 319, pilot = 120, Virginia = 146, and southern = 129, for a total of 953 with 849 open during the entire year. The percent of sites open all year for each of the regions was New England = 67 percent, mid-Atlantic (excluding pilot) = 98 percent, pilot = 99 percent,

Table 12—The average clicker count per sample day for each stratum adjusted to a 12-hour recreation day (this represents the average number of groups of all types of people exiting)

Site-type	Use-level	Sample days	Average	SE
		number		
TR	L	12	1.880	0.761
TR	M	9	0.506	0.375
TR	H	0	0.506[a]	0.375[a]
P	L	11	2.518	1.535
P	M	13	6.750	2.144
P	H	20	26.704	4.622
MU	L	7	13.689	9.603
MU	M	15	31.199	6.966
MU	H	21	51.939	17.436

SE = standard error; TR = trail/road; P = parking; MU = multiple use; L= low; M = medium; H = high.

[a] The TR–H stratum had no sample days so the average and SE are based on the TR–M stratum.

Table 13—Augmented counts for the ATCH from 9:00 a.m. until 4:00 or 5:00 p.m. for the pilot survey from June 1 to August 14, 2007

Date	Visitors	Hours	Date	Visitors	Hours
	- - - *number* - - -			- - - *number* - - -	
06/01/07	58	8	07/09/07	44	8
06/02/07	176	7	07/10/07	62	8
06/03/07	80	7	07/11/07	43	8
06/04/07	61	8	07/12/07	64	8
06/05/07	51	8	07/13/07	121	8
06/06/07	67	8	07/14/07	78	7
06/07/07	41	8	07/15/07	46	7
06/08/07	60	8	07/16/07	65	8
06/09/07	93	7	07/17/07	48	8
06/10/07	85	7	07/18/07	32	8
06/11/07	50	8	07/19/07	30	8
06/12/07	66	8	07/20/07	39	8
06/13/07	39	8	07/21/07	127	7
06/14/07	71	8	07/22/07	52	7
06/15/07	101	8	07/23/07	52	8
06/16/07	122	7	07/24/07	52	8
06/17/07	77	7	07/25/07	20	8
06/18/07	68	8	07/26/07	47	8
06/19/07	75	8	07/27/07	31	8
06/20/07	37	8	07/28/07	80	7
06/21/07	65	8	07/29/07	43	7
06/22/07	76	8	07/30/07	65	8
06/23/07	191	7	07/31/07	25	8
06/24/07	63	7	08/01/07	47	8
06/25/07	61	8	08/02/07	35	8
06/26/07	58	8	08/03/07	31	8
06/27/07	72	8	08/04/07	55	7
06/28/07	78	8	08/05/07	48	7
06/29/07	78	8	08/06/07	10	8
06/30/07	109	7	08/07/07	45	8
07/01/07	148	7	08/08/07	33	8
07/02/07	102	8	08/09/07	24	8
07/03/07	62	8	08/10/07	26	8
07/04/07	88	7	08/11/07	84	7
07/05/07	54	8	08/12/07	42	7
07/06/07	80	8	08/13/07	38	8
07/07/07	109	7	08/14/07	21	8
07/08/07	68	7			

ATCH = Appalachian Trail Conservancy Headquarters.

Virginia = 100 percent, and southern = 86 percent, with the overall being 89 percent. The prework spreadsheet for the site-type ATCH was based on the augmented site data obtained from the ATCH Office in Harpers Ferry, WV, for the entire year as explained previously. The site-type HF was increased to include the NPS Harpers Ferry National Historical Park monthly visitation estimates for the entire year. The TWE did not consist of any additional sampling but utilized the same sample selection and survey procedures used by the pilot survey.

Estimation Methodology

The TWE used the design-based approach and the model-based approach for estimation of the calibrating parameters. The model-based approach was particularly appealing because it allowed for an estimation of the ATCH–L and TR–H strata parameters which were needed for the TWE

visitation estimates despite no data for these strata being collected during the pilot survey. Relevant parameter estimates were derived using the relationships among all the site-types and use-levels developed with pilot survey data. However, the design-based approach used a somewhat more arbitrary method to obtain these missing values by merely substituting the parameter estimate from the closest use-level in the site-type.

Total visitation for the TWE for the entire 2007 year is defined by equation (13) except that *VISITS* is the total number of recreation visits on the entire AT from January 1 to December 31, 2007.

The standard site-type component which consists of sites in the strata composed of the TR, P, and MU site-types and all three use-levels L, M, and H is obtained by equation (15) where the summation is extended from $h = 1$ to 9 due to the inclusion of stratum TR–H. The TWE uses the N_h based on the total AT prework data (table 2), but the $\overline{P}_h$, $\overline{C}_h$, and $\overline{G}_h$ are obtained from the pilot survey based on equations (17), (19), and (22), respectively.

The augmented site-type ATCH data consisted of the 328 daily visitor tallies that the ATCH Office in Harpers Ferry, WV, obtained throughout the entire year (only pilot survey data is shown in table 13). Note that 37 days were missed due to official closure of the ATCH or due to poor weather conditions (table 17). This was combined with the estimates $\overline{P}_h$ and $\overline{G}_h$ obtained from the 6 sample site days taken during the pilot survey at the ATCH.

Let

N_h = total number of days that the ATCH has days in use-level $(h = L\,M\,H)$ during the entire year

n_h = number of days the ATCH tallied visitation for stratum h during the entire year

AS_{hi}^{ATCH} = the ATCH visitation tally on day i in use-level h

then, the average daily augmented site-type visitation tally in use-level h is the arithmetic mean as defined in equation (24). However, the estimated variance in equation (25) does not equal zero because n_h is less than N_h for use-level L and M, resulting in a nonvanishing finite population correction. The estimate for the ATCH for the TWE is obtained from equation (26) by extending the summation over all three use-levels and $\overline{P}_h$, $\overline{G}_h$, and $\overline{G}_h^a$ are calculated from the pilot survey data using equations (17), (22), and (27), respectively. As mentioned for the pilot survey, the variance equation (26) is quite complicated because it is a product of a constant and three variables as well as a ratio of a dependent variable. Previously, it was assumed that $\overline{G}_h^a$ was a constant, which is reasonable because its variance is quite small and it is highly correlated with $\overline{G}_h$. However, due to the nonvanishing finite population correction $\hat{V}\left(AS_h^{ATCH}\right) \neq 0$ for the TWE, a simplification cannot be made. Therefore, equation (29) is extended over all three use-levels and modified as

Table 14—The monthly augmented counts, strata weights, weighted $\overline{P}_i$, $\overline{G}_i$, and $\overline{G}_i^a$ estimates, and standard errors for the Harpers Ferry augmented data under the model-based approach

Month	Monthly augmented count	Strata weights			$\overline{P}_i$	$\overline{P}_i$ SE	$\overline{G}_i$	$\overline{G}_i$ SE	$\overline{G}_i^a$	$\overline{G}_i^a$ SE
		L	M	H						
	number									
Jan.	3,389	74	17	2	0.076	0.0393	2.48	0.500	2.85	0.194
Feb.	2,447	68	16	0	0.074	0.0400	2.48	0.508	2.85	0.198
Mar.	10,803	75	18	0	0.074	0.0399	2.48	0.507	2.85	0.197
Apr.	20,390	63	9	18	0.089	0.0346	2.49	0.440	2.83	0.171
May	32,597	66	9	18	0.088	0.0350	2.49	0.446	2.83	0.173
June	32,243	63	9	18	0.089	0.0346	2.49	0.440	2.83	0.171
July	40,522	63	10	20	0.091	0.0336	2.49	0.427	2.82	0.166
Aug.	26,520	69	8	16	0.085	0.0365	2.50	0.465	2.83	0.181
Sept.	28,160	57	11	22	0.096	0.0316	2.49	0.402	2.81	0.156
Oct.	32,243	66	9	18	0.088	0.0350	2.49	0.446	2.83	0.173
Nov.	15,383	71	17	2	0.076	0.0390	2.48	0.496	2.85	0.193
Dec.	5,211	56	23	14	0.094	0.0305	2.47	0.387	2.81	0.151
Total	249,908									

L = low; M = medium; H = high; SE = standard error.

$$\hat{V}\left(AS^{ATCH}\right) =$$

$$\sum_{h=L}^{H}\left(\frac{N_h}{\overline{G}_h^a}\right)^2\left\{\overline{P}_h^2\,\overline{AS_h^{ATCH}}^2\,\hat{V}\left(\overline{G}_h\right)+\overline{P}_h^2\,\overline{G}_h^2\,\hat{V}\left(\overline{AS_h^{ATCH}}\right)\right.$$

$$\left.+\overline{AS_h^{ATCH}}^2\,\overline{G}_h^2\,\hat{V}\left(\overline{P}_h\right)\right\}$$

$$-\sum_{h=L}^{H}\left(\frac{N_h}{\overline{G}_h^a}\right)^2\left\{\overline{P}_h^2\hat{V}\left(\overline{AS_h^{ATCH}}\right)\hat{V}\left(\overline{G}_h\right)\right. \qquad (43)$$

$$\left.+\overline{AS_h^{ATCH}}^2\hat{V}\left(\overline{P}_h\right)\hat{V}\left(\overline{G}_h\right)+\overline{G}_h^2\hat{V}\left(\overline{P}_h\right)\hat{V}\left(\overline{AS_h^{ATCH}}\right)\right\}$$

$$+\sum_{h=L}^{H}\left(\frac{N_h}{\overline{G}_h^a}\right)^2\left\{\hat{V}\left(\overline{P}_h\right)\hat{V}\left(\overline{AS_h^{ATCH}}\right)\right\}$$

The site-type HF sites consisted of the three sites located at Harpers Ferry (810, 811, and 813) and were estimated using the official monthly NPS Harpers Ferry National Historic Site visitation estimates as augmented site data as was done for the pilot survey (table 14). This provided visitation estimates based on data for the total 365 days at Harpers Ferry which was considered superior to visitation estimates derived from the 20 site days that were planned to be sampled during the pilot study. However, there were several limitations to using this augmented site data that had to be resolved. Recall that the NPS visitation included both AT and non-AT visits and was not stratified by use-level and was on a monthly basis. To resolve these problems required a monthly $\overline{P}_i$ derived from weighting the individual three

use-level estimates obtained from the pilot study for site-type HF by the monthly strata weights obtained from the prework spreadsheet data as shown in equation (30). To convert the NPS people tally to group tally a similar weighted mean of all group size was computed with equation (32). Also required was the monthly average group size for AT LERs defined by equation (34). The visitation for the TWE utilizes these monthly weighted estimates and the monthly NPS augmented site-type visitation estimate and is defined by modifying equation (36) to extend over all 12 months with $k = 1$ for all months.

The only special event identified for the TWE was Foundry Day at Boiling Springs, PA, on June 2, 2007. Thus, the estimate from the pilot was simply used in this instance.

Extrapolation Results

The visitation estimates were calculated based on the previously described methodology using the calibrating parameter estimates obtained by the pilot survey. Estimates were based on the design-based and model-based approaches for comparison purposes. The estimates based on each stratum along with standard errors, CV, and 95-percent confidence intervals are shown in table 18. The TWE is based on data from the pilot survey and, thus, the relationships discussed previously are generally the same here.

The TWE estimates for both approaches are shown in table 16 for the standard site-types, the augmented site-type ATCH, the augmented site-type HF, the special event, and the total. The total visitation for the entire AT using the model-based approach was 1,948,701 with a 95-percent confidence interval of 1,172,146 to 2,725,256.

Table 15—Pilot survey visitation (site-type HF represents the summation over all use-levels and all three sites because monthly augmented data were used)

Site-type	Use-level	Total site days	Visits per day	Total visits	Standard error	Coefficient of variation	Lower 95 CI	Upper 95 CI
		- - - - - - - - - *number* - - - - - - - - - -				*percent*		
TR	L	3,624	2.8	10,217	8,505	83	−6,453	26,887
TR	L	3,624	2.6	9,493	5,318	56	−931	19,918
TR	M	651	0.5	329	244	74	−150	808
TR	M	651	0.7	484	390	80	−279	1,248
TR	H	0	—	—	—	—	—	—
TR	H	0	—	—	—	—	—	—
P	L	1,781	3.9	6,923	4,792	69	−2,469	16,315
P	L	1,781	4.7	8,422	5,355	64	−2,073	18,917
P	M	689	12.9	8,893	4,710	53	−339	18,125
P	M	689	13.2	9,127	3,094	34	3,063	15,191
P	H	80	58.8	4,704	1,072	23	2,603	6,806
P	H	80	58.2	4,653	861	19	2,965	6,341
MU	L	1,161	9.7	11,269	8,778	78	−5,936	28,475
MU	L	1,161	7.3	8,430	6,217	74	−3,756	20,616
MU	M	542	18.0	9,732	4,331	45	1,243	18,221
MU	M	542	21.0	11,382	3,148	28	5,213	17,551
MU	H	167	43.1	7,205	3,241	45	852	13,557
MU	H	167	42.4	7,078	2,518	36	2,144	12,012
ATCH	L	0	—	—	—	—	—	—
ATCH	L	0	—	—	—	—	—	—
ATCH	M	14	17.3	242	121	50	5	479
ATCH	M	14	14.5	203	59	29	87	318
ATCH	H	61	29.6	1,806	521	29	785	2,827
ATCH	H	61	31.0	1,892	469	25	973	2,811
HF	L, M, H	75	34.8	2,614	499	19	1,636	3,591
HF	L, M, H	75	89.5	6,716	1,740	26	3,306	10,125
Special	—	—	—	3,032	1,765	58	−427	6,491
Total design-based estimates				66,967	15,122	23	37,328	96,605
Total model-based estimates				70,912	11,344	16	48,678	93,146

Note: The first line of each pair represents the design-based estimates and the second the model-based estimates.
— = no data; CI = confidence intervals; TR = trail/road; P = parking; MU = multiple use; ATCH = Appalachian Trail Conservancy Headquarters; HF = Harpers Ferry; L= low; M = medium; H = high.

The CV was 20 percent which is considered quite good especially for the low level of sampling that was performed. The bulk of the visitation (99 percent) could be attributed to the standard sites because any additional sites like the site-types HF and ATCH and the special event were not identified outside of the pilot survey area.

The TWE using the design-based approach yields similar findings to the model-based approach. The overall visitation estimate with the design-based approach is 1,925,044 with a 95-percent confidence interval of 886,457 to 2,963,630, and a CV of 28 percent.

Table 16—The final visitation estimates for the pilot survey and the trailwide extrapolation for the entire AT

Estimate	Total visits	Standard error	Coefficient of variation	Lower 95 CI	Upper 95 CI
	number				
Design-based approach					
Pilot Standard	59,273	15,001	25	29,872	88,674
Pilot ATCH	2,048	535	26	1,000	3,096
Pilot HF	2,614	499	19	1,636	3,591
Pilot SE	3,032	1,765	58	−427	6,491
Pilot total	66,967	15,122	23	37,328	96,605
Model-based approach					
Pilot Standard	59,070	11,060	19	37,392	80,747
Pilot ATCH	2,095	472	23	1,169	3,021
Pilot HF	6,716	1,740	26	3,306	10,125
Pilot SE	3,032	1,765	58	−427	6,491
Pilot total	70,912	11,344	16	48,678	93,146
Design-based approach					
AT Standard	1,908,847	529,885	28	870,272	2,947,423
AT ATCH	5,720	1,468	26	2,844	8,597
AT HF	7,444	788	11	5,899	8,989
AT SE	3,032	1,765	58	−427	6,491
AT total	1,925,044	529,891	28	886,457	2,963,630
Model-based approach					
AT Standard	1,921,047	396,187	21	1,144,522	2,697,573
AT ATCH	5,239	916	17	3,444	7,034
AT HF	19,383	2,785	14	13,923	24,842
AT SE	3,032	1,765	58	−427	6,491
AT total	1,948,701	396,201	20	1,172,146	2,725,256

AT = Appalachian National Scenic Trail; CI = confidence intervals; ATCH = Appalachian Trail Conservancy Headquarters; HF = Harpers Ferry; SE = special event.

Table 17—The days when the ATCH Office in Harpers Ferry, WV, was officially closed or closed due to weather (some closed days had visitor counts because they were opened partially or closed early due to bad weather conditions)

Month	Officially closed (date)	Due to weather (date)
January	1, 6, 7, 13, 14, 15, 20, 21, 27, 28	18
February	3, 4, 10, 11, 17, 18, 19, 24, 25	8, 13, 14
March	3, 4, 10, 11, 17, 18, 24, 25	
November	22	
December	22, 23, 25, 29, 30	

Part III—Conclusions and Limitations

The main objective of this research was to develop a prototype survey design that could be used for estimating visitation on long, linear trails and apply this prototype to a major portion of the AT. The survey design framework produced a sampling frame based on exit sites that can be stratified by site-type and expected use-level or exit volume. It is believed that this structure could easily and efficiently be applied to other segments of the AT, as well as other long trails, with only minor modifications such as additional site-types and/or use-levels for both standard and augmented sites, and special events. The results of the pilot survey, using the model-based approach, yielded a visitation estimate of 70,912, with a 95-percent confidence interval of 48,678 to 93,146, for the 75-day time period in 2007 from Harpers Ferry to 10 trail miles north of Boiling Springs, PA, at the Scott Farm.

Satisfying a second major research objective, these model-based results were extrapolated to produce an annual 2007 visitation estimate for entire AT of 1,948,701 with a 95-percent confidence interval of 1,172,146 to 2,725,256. This estimate is about 50 percent less than the previously reported annual AT visitation of 3 to 4 million (Appalachian Trail Conservancy 2009, National Park Service 2009a). Although the annual visitation estimate for the entire trail produced by our methodology is an extrapolation from the pilot survey, and is, thus, dependent on a number of assumptions (see the "Overview" section, pages 36-37), it is scientifically defensible, and the methodology provides a structure for examining the various assumptions through sensitivity analyses.

The third objective of this project was to provide a preliminary estimate of the resources required for a survey of the entire Appalachian Trail for a full year as opposed to an extrapolation based on the pilot survey. Although it is possible to determine the number of sample site days required to achieve a specified level of precision given the total number of site days and level of variability for each stratum, we are only providing a rough guideline here. This is because the variances were at times poorly estimated, especially for the TR site-type where the use-levels were based on low-sample size or for TR–H, not estimated at all.

First, consider that 25 sample site days are needed to provide an estimate of the strata means for each of the 3 use-levels in each of the site-types TR, P, and MU that are remotely located along the AT. Generally, a sample size of 25 is considered appropriate for a sample mean because this is where the *t*-distribution closely approaches the normal distribution and asymptotic properties of estimators begin to be achieved. Theoretically, a stratum like TR–L that has more total site days and possibly greater variability should have greater allocation than a stratum like MU–H.

However, the visitation in TR–L is very low, and it is felt more important to allocate more resources where the visitation is higher as in MU–H which will provide more interviews that are not only useful for the visitation estimate but also for any of the other estimates that are addressed in the survey questionnaire. It is important to also keep in mind that at these sites where daily visitation may be low, especially site-type TR, some of the 25 site days may have no visitors and, hence, contribute no data for estimating some of the visitation parameters. Thus, allocating an equal sample size of 25 site days appears to be a good compromise between theoretical and practical considerations. The other two site-types, ATCH and HF, are both located in Harpers Ferry, WV, and consist of only one and three sites, respectively. Thus, it was felt that 30 site days for each of these site-types, 10 per use-level, would be adequate. There was one special event in the pilot study, but the total number along the entire AT was unknown. Thus, for lack of information, we assume there is one additional special event per each of the four AT regions, yielding five special events in total. Based on this allocation, it is estimated that 290 sample site days distributed throughout the year would be adequate for a total annual AT visitation estimate.

The cost associated with sampling 290 site days and the analysis of the data consists of several components. Assuming an 8-hour survey day at $15 per hour and transportation costs of $20, gives a total cost of $140 per day or $40,600 for all 290 site days. The data entry costs consist of manually entering data from the daily summary forms and the interview forms for each site day at a rate of $15 per hour. The cost of entering all the daily summary forms is $435 assuming an entry rate of 10 per hour. Assuming 20 interviews per site day, the interview forms, which are a little longer and can be entered 8 per hour, would cost $10,875. Additional effort is needed for data editing, adjustments to the estimation computer program, analysis, and report writing, totaling $30,000. Fortunately, the questionnaire development and stratification of the entire AT has already been accomplished and will entail no further costs. Travel, logistics, supplies, postage, and other miscellaneous items total an additional $5,000. Thus, an approximate estimate for performing an entire annual AT visitation survey would be $86,910. There is potential to reduce this by a substantial amount by not having to pay interviewers for their labor and data entry if sufficient volunteers could be obtained. With surveying spread over the entire year and trail, the concentration of interviewer work would also be spread out and this would probably be more conducive to obtaining volunteers.

The distinction between standard and augmented sites proved quite useful for separating groups of estimators and resulted into more efficient estimators. Augmented sites are advantageous because they contain a "known" quantity that can be exploited to produce a less variable visitation

Table 18—Trailwide extrapolation visitation (site-type HF represents the summation over all use-levels and all three sites because monthly augmented data were used)

Site-type	Use-level	Total site days	Visits per day	Total visits	Standard error	Coefficient of variation	Lower 95 CI	Upper 95 CI
		- - - - - - -	number	- - - - - - - - -				
TR	L	184,988	2.8	521,552	434,145	83	−329,372	1,372,476
TR	L	184,988	2.6	484,593	271,482	56	−47,512	1,016,699
TR	M	8,112	0.5	4,103	3,044	74	−1,864	10,069
TR	M	8,112	0.7	6,033	4,854	80	−3,480	15,547
TR	H	9,490	0.5	4,800	3,561	74	−2,181	11,780
TR	H	9,490	0.8	7,957	6,351	80	−4,490	20,404
P	L	81,429	3.9	316,510	219,085	69	−112,896	745,916
P	L	81,429	4.7	385,048	244,821	64	−94,801	864,898
P	M	19,140	12.9	247,039	130,846	53	−9,420	503,497
P	M	19,140	13.2	253,553	85,944	34	85,102	422,004
P	H	8,625	58.8	507,200	115,581	23	280,661	733,739
P	H	8,625	58.2	501,664	92,837	19	319,704	683,625
MU	L	13,279	9.7	128,893	100,403	78	−67,898	325,684
MU	L	13,279	7.3	96,417	71,110	74	−42,959	235,792
MU	M	3,028	18.0	54,372	24,197	45	6,946	101,797
MU	M	3,028	21.0	63,589	17,585	28	29,123	98,055
MU	H	2,883	43.1	124,380	55,953	45	14,712	234,049
MU	H	2,883	42.4	122,193	43,462	36	37,008	207,377
ATCH	L	120	5.6	676	338	50	15	1,338
ATCH	L	120	3.9	467	177	38	120	815
ATCH	M	157	15.5	2,431	1,213	50	53	4,808
ATCH	M	157	13.0	2,033	589	29	837	3,188
ATCH	H	88	29.7	2,613	754	29	1,136	4,091
ATCH	H	88	31.1	2,739	678	25	1,409	4,046
HF	L, M, H	365	20.4	7,444	788	11	5,899	8,989
HF	L, M, H	365	53.1	19,383	2,785	14	13,923	24,842
Special	—	—	—	3,032	1,765	58	−427	6,491
Total design-based estimates				1,925,044	529,891	28	886,457	2,963,630
Total model-based estimates				1,948,701	396,201	20	1,172,146	2,725,256

Note: The first line of each pair represents the design-based estimates and the second the model-based estimates.
— = Entries do not apply to the Special site-type. HF = Harpers Ferry; TR = trail/road; P = parking; MU = multiple use; ATCH = Appalachian Trail Conservancy Headquarters; L = low; M = medium; H = high.

estimate based in part on data that is collected outside the survey. In addition, this can lead to more optimal use of limited resources. In the present study, there were only two augmented site-types, HF and ATCH, but in other trail surveys there may be numerous ones depending on the level of auxiliary information that is known about the trail. The HF augmented site-type illustrated use of auxiliary data consisting of NPS monthly visitation estimates, while the ATCH augmented site-type was based on very accurate daily visitation tallies obtained from the ATC. These illustrated two different methodologies to convert these augmented site-types to appropriate visitation estimates. Undoubtedly, other sections of the AT, or other trails in general, could have different augmented site-types such as fee tickets, parking lot counts, or mandatory registration that would require further adaptation of these methods for conversion.

There was only one special event identified in the survey and the application of mark-recapture methods commonly used with wildlife population was found useful in estimating this visitation. The value of isolating a special event instead of simply including the 3 site days in the MU-L stratum and the 2 site days in the MU–H stratum resulted in 3,032 visits instead of $3(7.3)+2(42.4)=106.7$ visits obtained using the relevant standard site-type information. This difference emphasizes the importance of identifying all special events in future surveys. Obviously, special events require knowledge of the site(s), and other innovative techniques besides mark-recapture methods may have to be employed. It is likely that some special events on trails may actually provide opportunity for complete censuses of LERs based on the specific administrative or coordination activities associated with the particular events.

One of the major problems in trail visitation estimation is that onsite sampling often results in sampled site days having low or no visitation, thus yielding no data for estimation of the important scale parameters $\overline{P}_h$, $\overline{G}_h$, and $\overline{G}_h^a$. Such low sampling intensity not only results in erratic estimates of these parameters with large variability as shown in this report, but is the reason why the visitation estimators are based on the product of their means instead of the mean of their individual daily product.

The model-based approach was used here in an attempt to mitigate the effect of small sample sizes on the design-based estimator. Results for the parameter estimates reveal several justifications for preferring the model-based approach over the design-based approach. First, limited resources can result in low-sampling intensity for certain strata which increases the risk of erratic estimates for the design-based approach. This is alleviated to a certain extent with the model-based approach because the data are combined, the relationship between site-type and use-level is modeled, and then the individual strata estimates are obtained from the model. Second, the model-based approach smoothes the calibration parameter estimates so that inconsistencies

are eliminated or mitigated. For instance, if a parameter increases with increasing use-level for a given site-type, it probably exhibits this pattern for the other site-types. The design-based approach does not have this property because the individual strata estimates are not linked via a common model. Third, the standard errors of the parameter estimates are substantially smaller with the model-based approach because all the data are combined and used jointly in the estimation process. Alternatively, the design-based approach estimates a stratum's parameter based only on the data observed in that stratum, which results in a smaller sample size and, consequently, a larger standard error.

Despite the advantages of the model-based approach when the sampling intensity is low, the design-based approach is preferred when adequate sampling is affordable and has been achieved. In recreation use studies, this is rarely the case. With the design-based approach, the estimate for a given stratum is independent of the other strata and is capable of reflecting its individual characteristics and properties. It does not rely on a model which may or may not assume interaction between site-type and use-level.

Future research will hopefully allow sampling across the entire spatial and temporal range of the AT so that extrapolation is unnecessary to estimate overall annual visitation. Parameter and visitation estimates derived from the pilot survey, along with the trailwide site day classification which was part of this research, will be fundamental to making a future trailwide sampling and visitation estimate economically feasible.

Literature Cited

Appalachian Trail Conservancy. 2009. Through hiking facts and statistics. http://www.appalachiantrail.org/site/c.jkLXJ8MQKtH/b.715465/k.9731/Hike_The_Trail.htm. [Date accessed: January 6, 2009].

Bergstrom, J.C.; Teasley, R.J.; Cordell, H.K. [and others]. 1996. Effects of reservoir aquatic plant management on recreational expenditures and regional economic activity. Journal of Agricultural and Applied Economics. 28: 409–422.

Bowker, J.M.; Bergstrom, J.C.; Gill, J. 2007. Estimating the economic value and impacts of recreational trails: a case study of the Virginia Creeper Rail Trail. Tourism Economics. 13: 241–260.

Bowker, J.M.; Bergstrom, J.C.; Gill, J.A. 2004. The Virginia Creeper Trail: an assessment of user demographics, preferences, and economics. http://www.srs.fs.usda.gov/recreation/VCT.pdf. [Date accessed: January 6, 2009].

Cochran, W.G. 1977. Sampling techniques. 3d ed. New York: John Wiley. 428 p.

English, D.B.K.; Kocis, S.M.; Arnold, J.R. [and others]. 2003. The effectiveness of visitation proxy variables in improving recreation use estimates for the USDA Forest Service. Journal for Nature Conservation. 11: 332–338.

English, D.B.K.; Kocis, S.M.; Zarnoch, S.J.; Arnold, J.R. 2002. Forest Service national visitor use monitoring process: research method documentation. Gen. Tech. Rep. SRS–57. Asheville, NC: U.S. Department of Agriculture Forest Service, Southern Research Station. 14 p.

Goodman, L.A. 1960. On the exact variance of products. Journal of the American Statistical Association. 55(292): 708–713.

Gregoire, T.G.; Buhyoff, G.J. 1999. Sampling and estimating recreational use. Gen. Tech. Rep. PNW–456. Portland, OR: U.S. Department of Agriculture Forest Service, Pacific Northwest Research Station. 39 p.

Jacobi, C. 2003. A census of hiking trail use in Acadia National Park August 5 and 6, 2003. http://www.nps.gov/archive/rm/docs/pdf/visitoruse/cens2003.pdf. [Date accessed: February 5, 2009].

James, G.; Schreuder, H. 1971. Estimating use on the San Gorgonio Wilderness Area. Journal of Forestry. 68(8): 490–493.

Kyle, G.; Graefe, A.; Manning, R.; Bacon, J. 2004. Predictors of behavioral loyalty among hikers along the Appalachian Trail. Leisure Sciences. 26: 99–118.

Lindsey, P.; Lindsey, G. 2004. Using pedestrian count models to estimate urban trail traffic. Journal of Regional Analysis and Policy. 34(1): 51–68.

Manning, R.E.; Valliere, W.; Bacon, J.J. [and others]. 2000. Use and users of the Appalachian Trail: a source book. http://www.nps.gov/appa/parkmgmt/upload/Main_Report-2.pdf. [Date accessed: February 5, 2009].

National Park Service. 2008. Harpers Ferry NHP reports: visitation by month/year. http://www.nature.nps.gov/stats/park.cfm. [Date accessed: February 5, 2009].

National Park Service. 2009a. Appalachian National Scenic Trail: news. http://www.nps.gov/appa/naturescience/index.htm. [Date accessed: January 16, 2009].

National Park Service. 2009b. Director's order #82: public use data collecting and reporting program. http://www.nps.gov/policy/DOrders/DO-82draft.htm. [Date accessed: January 16, 2009].

SAS Institute Inc. 2004. SAS/STAT® 9.1 user's guide. Cary, NC: SAS Institute Inc. 5,121 p.

Seber, G.A.F. 1982. The estimation of animal abundance and related parameters. 2d ed. Caldwell, NJ: The Blackburn Press. 654 p.

Stynes, D. 1996. October use patterns on Lansing's Riverfront Trail. http://www.msu.edu/course/prr/389/trail96.doc. [Date accessed: February 5, 2009].

White, Eric M.; Zarnoch, Stanley J.; English, Donald B.K. 2007. Area-specific recreation use estimation using the national visitor use monitoring program data. Res. Note PNW–557. Portland, OR: U.S. Department of Agriculture Forest Service, Pacific Northwest Research Station. 26 p.

Wolter, S.A.; Lindsey, G. 2001. Summary report: Indiana trails study-a study of trails in 6 Indiana cities. http://atfiles.org/files/pdf/INtrailsstudy01.pdf. [Date accessed: February 5, 2009].

Zarnoch, S.J.; Kocis, S.M.; Cordell, H.K.; English, D.B.K. 2002. A pilot sampling design for estimating outdoor recreation site visits on the national forests. Res. Pap. SRS–29. Asheville, NC: U.S. Department of Agriculture Forest Service, Southern Research Station. 20 p.

Appendix A

List of Acronyms and Abbreviations

AT = Appalachian National Scenic Trail

ATC = Appalachian Trail Conservancy

ATCH = Appalachian Trail Conservancy Headquarters site-type

CI = Confidence intervals

CV = Coefficient of variation

GIS = Geographical Information System

H = High use-level

HF = Harpers Ferry site-type

L = Low use-level

LER = Last-exiting recreationist

M = Medium use-level

MU = Multiple use site-type

NPS = National Park Service

NVUM = National Visitor Use Monitoring

P = Parking site-type

PSU = Primary sampling unit

SE = Standard error

SSU = Secondary sampling unit

TR = Trail/road site-type

TWE = Trailwide extrapolation

USFS = U.S. Forest Service

The pilot survey prework spreadsheet consists of all the sites classified into site-types and use-levels for the entire 2007 calendar year. The pilot survey actually used only those site days from June 1 through August 14, 2007. The site names that correspond to the site numbers can be found in table 1.

Site number	Site type	Use-level	Begin	End	Mon.	Tues.	Wed.	Thurs.	Fri.	Sat.	Sun.	Holiday
0	ATCH	L	101	330	1	1	1	1	1	1	1	
0	ATCH	M	331	430	1	1	1	1	1			
0	ATCH	H	331	430						1	1	
0	ATCH	M	501	531	1	1	1	1	1			
0	ATCH	H	501	531						1	1	1
0	ATCH	H	601	731	1	1	1	1	1	1	1	1
0	ATCH	M	801	930	1	1	1	1	1	1	1	1
0	ATCH	M	1001	1031	1	1	1	1	1			1
0	ATCH	H	1001	1031						1	1	
0	ATCH	M	1101	1130	1	1	1	1	1	1	1	1
0	ATCH	L	1201	1231	1	1	1	1	1	1	1	1
809	TR	L	101	1231	1	1	1	1	1	1	1	1
810	HF	L	102	1224	1	1	1	1	1			
810	HF	M	102	331						1	1	
810	HF	M	1101	1224						1	1	
810	HF	H	101	101	1							
810	HF	H	401	1031						1	1	
810	HF	H	1225	1231	1	1	1	1	1	1	1	
810	HF	H	101	1231								1
811	HF	L	102	331	1	1	1	1	1	1	1	
811	HF	L	401	1031	1	1	1	1	1			
811	HF	L	1101	1224	1	1	1	1	1	1	1	
811	HF	M	101	101	1							
811	HF	M	401	1031						1	1	
811	HF	M	1225	1231	1	1	1	1	1	1	1	
811	HF	M	101	1231								1
812	HF	L	101	1231	1	1	1	1	1	1	1	1
813	HF	L	102	1224	1	1	1	1	1			
813	HF	M	102	331						1	1	
813	HF	M	1101	1224						1	1	
813	HF	H	101	101	1							
813	HF	H	401	1031						1	1	
813	HF	H	1225	1231	1	1	1	1	1	1	1	
813	HF	H	101	1231								1
814	TR	L	101	1231	1	1	1	1	1	1	1	1
816	P	L	102	331	1	1	1	1	1	1	1	
816	P	L	401	1031	1	1	1	1	1			
816	P	L	1101	1224	1	1	1	1	1	1	1	
816	P	M	101	101	1							
816	P	M	401	1031						1	1	
816	P	M	1225	1231	1	1	1	1	1	1	1	
816	P	M	101	1231								1
817	TR	L	101	1231	1	1	1	1	1	1	1	1
819	P	L	102	1224	1	1	1	1	1			
819	P	M	102	331						1	1	
819	P	M	1101	1224						1	1	
819	P	H	101	101	1							
819	P	H	401	1031						1	1	

continued

Appendix B

The pilot survey prework spreadsheet consists of all the sites classified into site-types and use-levels for the entire 2007 calendar year. The pilot survey actually used only those site days from June 1 through August 14, 2007. The site names that correspond to the site numbers can be found in table 1 (continued)

Site number	Site-type	Use-level	Begin	End	Mon.	Tues.	Wed.	Thurs.	Fri.	Sat.	Sun.	Holiday
819	P	H	1225	1231	1	1	1	1	1	1	1	
819	P	H	101	1231								1
828	MU	L	102	331	1	1	1	1	1	1	1	
828	MU	L	401	1031	1	1	1	1	1			
828	MU	L	1101	1224	1	1	1	1	1	1	1	
828	MU	M	101	101	1							
828	MU	M	401	1031						1	1	
828	MU	M	1225	1231	1	1	1	1	1	1	1	
828	MU	M	101	1231								1
827	MU	L	101	1231	1	1	1	1	1	1	1	1
825	MU	L	102	1224	1	1	1	1	1			
825	MU	M	102	331						1	1	
825	MU	M	1101	1224						1	1	
825	MU	H	101	101	1							
825	MU	H	401	1031						1	1	
825	MU	H	1225	1231	1	1	1	1	1	1	1	
825	MU	H	101	1231								1
829	TR	L	101	1231	1	1	1	1	1	1	1	1
832	P	L	101	331	1	1	1	1	1	1	1	
832	P	L	401	1031	1	1	1	1	1			
832	P	L	1101	1231	1	1	1	1	1	1	1	
832	P	M	401	1031						1	1	
832	P	M	101	1231								1
833	TR	L	101	1231	1	1	1	1	1	1	1	1
834	P	L	401	430	1	1	1	1	1	1	1	
834	P	L	801	1130	1	1	1	1	1	1	1	1
834	P	M	501	731	1	1	1	1	1	1	1	1
835	P	L	101	331	1	1	1	1	1	1	1	
835	P	L	401	1031	1	1	1	1	1			
835	P	L	1101	1231	1	1	1	1	1	1	1	
835	P	M	401	1031						1	1	
835	P	M	101	1231								1
836	P	L	101	228	1	1	1	1	1	1	1	
836	P	L	301	531	1	1	1	1	1			
836	P	L	1001	1031	1	1	1	1	1			
836	P	L	1101	1231	1	1	1	1	1	1	1	
836	P	L	704	704								1
836	P	L	903	903								1
836	P	L	1122	1122								1
836	P	M	301	531						1	1	
836	P	M	1001	1031						1	1	
836	P	M	601	930	1	1	1	1	1	1	1	
836	P	M	528	528								1
836	P	M	1008	1008								1
838	TR	L	101	1231	1	1	1	1	1	1	1	1
839	MU	L	101	1231	1	1	1	1	1	1	1	1
841	MU	L	101	228	1	1	1	1	1	1	1	1
841	MU	L	301	430	1	1	1	1	1			
841	MU	L	901	1031	1	1	1	1	1			

continued

The pilot survey prework spreadsheet consists of all the sites classified into site-types and use-levels for the entire 2007 calendar year. The pilot survey actually used only those site days from June 1 through August 14, 2007. The site names that correspond to the site numbers can be found in table 1 (continued)

Site number	Site-type	Use-level	Begin	End	Mon.	Tues.	Wed.	Thurs.	Fri.	Sat.	Sun.	Holiday
841	MU	L	1101	1231	1	1	1	1	1	1	1	1
841	MU	M	301	430						1	1	
841	MU	M	501	630	1	1	1	1	1			
841	MU	H	501	630						1	1	
841	MU	H	701	831	1	1	1	1	1	1	1	
841	MU	H	901	1031						1	1	
841	MU	H	528	1008								1
840	MU	L	101	1231	1	1	1	1	1	1	1	1
842	MU	L	101	1231	1	1	1	1	1	1	1	1
844	P	L	101	1231	1	1	1	1	1	1	1	1
846	TR	L	101	1231	1	1	1	1	1	1	1	1
848	TR	L	101	1231	1	1	1	1	1	1	1	1
849	P	L	101	228	1	1	1	1	1	1	1	
849	P	L	301	531	1	1	1	1	1			
849	P	L	1101	1231	1	1	1	1	1			
849	P	M	301	531						1	1	
849	P	M	601	1031	1	1	1	1				
849	P	M	1101	1231						1	1	
849	P	H	601	1031					1	1	1	
849	P	H	101	1231								1
853	TR	L	101	331	1	1	1	1	1	1	1	
853	TR	L	1101	1231	1	1	1	1	1	1	1	
853	TR	L	401	1031	1	1	1	1	1			
853	TR	M	401	1031						1	1	
853	TR	M	401	1031								1
853	TR	M	1122	1122				1	1			1
857	TR	L	101	1231	1	1	1	1	1	1	1	1
864	P	L	101	331	1	1	1	1	1	1	1	
864	P	L	401	1031	1	1	1	1	1			
864	P	L	1101	1231	1	1	1	1	1	1	1	
864	P	M	401	1031						1	1	
864	P	M	101	1231								1
865	P	L	101	331	1	1	1	1	1	1	1	
865	P	L	401	1031	1	1	1	1	1			
865	P	L	1101	1231	1	1	1	1	1	1	1	
865	P	M	401	1031						1	1	
865	P	M	101	1231								1
867	TR	L	101	331	1	1	1	1	1	1	1	
867	TR	L	401	1031	1	1	1	1	1			
867	TR	L	1101	1231	1	1	1	1	1	1	1	
867	TR	M	401	1031						1	1	
867	TR	M	101	1231								1
869	TR	L	101	1231	1	1	1	1	1	1	1	1
872	P	L	101	1231	1	1	1	1	1	1	1	1
874	TR	L	101	1231	1	1	1	1	1	1	1	1
875	P	L	101	331	1	1	1	1	1	1	1	
875	P	L	1101	1131	1	1	1	1	1			
875	P	L	1201	1231	1	1	1	1	1	1	1	
875	P	M	401	531	1	1	1	1	1	1	1	

continued

Appendix B

The pilot survey prework spreadsheet consists of all the sites classified into site-types and use-levels for the entire 2007 calendar year. The pilot survey actually used only those site days from June 1 through August 14, 2007. The site names that correspond to the site numbers can be found in table 1 (continued)

Site number	Site-type	Use-level	Begin	End	Mon.	Tues.	Wed.	Thurs.	Fri.	Sat.	Sun.	Holiday
875	P	M	601	1031	1	1	1	1	1			
875	P	M	1101	1130						1	1	
875	P	H	601	1031						1	1	
875	P	H	101	1231								1
878	MU	L	101	331	1	1	1	1	1	1	1	
878	MU	L	1101	1231	1	1	1	1	1	1	1	1
878	MU	L	401	430	1	1	1	1	1			
878	MU	L	1001	1031	1	1	1	1	1			
878	MU	M	401	430						1	1	
878	MU	M	1001	1031						1	1	1
878	MU	M	501	930	1	1	1	1	1	1	1	1
881	TR	L	101	1231	1	1	1	1	1	1	1	1
884	TR	L	101	1231	1	1	1	1	1	1	1	1
887	TR	L	101	1231	1	1	1	1	1	1	1	1
888	P	L	101	630	1	1	1	1	1			
888	P	L	901	1231	1	1	1	1	1			
888	P	M	101	630						1	1	
888	P	M	701	831	1	1	1	1	1	1	1	
888	P	M	901	1231						1	1	
888	P	M	101	1231								1
890	P	L	101	331	1	1	1	1	1	1	1	
890	P	L	401	1031	1	1	1	1	1			
890	P	L	1101	1231	1	1	1	1	1	1	1	
890	P	M	401	1031						1	1	
890	P	M	101	1231								1
891	TR	L	101	1231	1	1	1	1	1	1	1	1
893	TR	L	101	1231	1	1	1	1	1	1	1	1
897	P	L	101	331	1	1	1	1	1	1	1	
897	P	L	401	1031	1	1	1	1	1			
897	P	L	1101	1231	1	1	1	1	1	1	1	
897	P	M	401	1031						1	1	
897	P	M	101	1231								1
899	TR	L	101	430	1	1	1	1	1	1	1	
899	TR	L	501	630	1	1	1	1	1			
899	TR	L	901	1031	1	1	1	1	1			
899	TR	L	1101	1231	1	1	1	1	1	1	1	
899	TR	M	501	630						1	1	
899	TR	M	701	831	1	1	1	1	1	1	1	
899	TR	M	901	1031						1	1	
899	TR	M	101	1231								1
901	P	L	101	331	1	1	1	1	1	1	1	
901	P	L	401	1031	1	1	1	1	1			
901	P	L	1101	1231	1	1	1	1	1	1	1	
901	P	M	401	1031						1	1	
901	P	M	101	1231								1
903	P	L	101	331	1	1	1	1	1	1	1	
903	P	L	401	1031	1	1	1	1	1			
903	P	L	1101	1231	1	1	1	1	1	1	1	
903	P	M	401	1031						1	1	

continued

Appendix B

The pilot survey prework spreadsheet consists of all the sites classified into site-types and use-levels for the entire 2007 calendar year. The pilot survey actually used only those site days from June 1 through August 14, 2007. The site names that correspond to the site numbers can be found in table 1 (continued)

Site number	Site-type	Use-level	Begin	End	Mon.	Tues.	Wed.	Thurs.	Fri.	Sat.	Sun.	Holiday
903	P	M	101	1231								1
904	TR	L	101	1231	1	1	1	1	1	1	1	1
905	P	L	101	331	1	1	1	1	1	1	1	
905	P	L	401	1031	1	1	1	1	1			
905	P	L	1101	1231	1	1	1	1	1	1	1	
905	P	M	401	1031						1	1	
905	P	M	101	1231								1
908	TR	L	101	1231	1	1	1	1	1	1	1	1
909	TR	L	101	430	1	1	1	1	1	1	1	
909	TR	L	501	630	1	1	1	1	1			
909	TR	L	901	1031	1	1	1	1	1			
909	TR	L	1101	1231	1	1	1	1	1	1	1	
909	TR	M	501	630						1	1	
909	TR	M	701	831	1	1	1	1	1	1	1	
909	TR	M	901	1031						1	1	
909	TR	M	101	1231								1
910	P	L	101	331	1	1	1	1	1	1	1	
910	P	L	401	1031	1	1	1	1	1			
910	P	L	1101	1231	1	1	1	1	1	1	1	
910	P	M	401	1031						1	1	
910	P	M	101	1231								1
913	TR	L	101	1231	1	1	1	1	1	1	1	1
914	MU	L	101	1231	1	1	1	1	1	1	1	1
915	MU	L	101	1231	1	1	1	1	1	1	1	1
916	MU	L	102	331	1	1	1	1	1	1	1	
916	MU	L	401	1031	1	1	1	1	1			
916	MU	L	1101	1224	1	1	1	1	1	1	1	
916	MU	M	101	101	1							
916	MU	M	401	1031						1	1	
916	MU	M	1225	1231	1	1	1	1	1	1	1	
916	MU	M	101	1231								1
917	MU	L	102	331	1	1	1	1	1	1	1	
917	MU	L	401	1031	1	1	1	1	1			
917	MU	L	1101	1224	1	1	1	1	1	1	1	
917	MU	M	101	101	1							
917	MU	M	401	1031						1	1	
917	MU	M	1225	1231	1	1	1	1	1	1	1	
917	MU	M	101	1231								1
919	MU	L	101	331	1	1	1	1	1	1	1	
919	MU	L	401	531	1	1	1	1	1			
919	MU	L	901	1130	1	1	1	1	1			
919	MU	L	1201	1231	1	1	1	1	1	1	1	
919	MU	M	401	531						1	1	
919	MU	M	601	831	1	1	1	1	1			
919	MU	M	1001	1130						1	1	
919	MU	H	601	930						1	1	
919	MU	H	101	1231								1
920	MU	L	101	1231	1	1	1	1	1	1	1	1
921	MU	L	101	1231	1	1	1	1	1	1	1	1

continued

The pilot survey prework spreadsheet consists of all the sites classified into site-types and use-levels for the entire 2007 calendar year. The pilot survey actually used only those site days from June 1 through August 14, 2007. The site names that correspond to the site numbers can be found in table 1 (continued)

Site number	Site-type	Use-level	Begin	End	Mon.	Tues.	Wed.	Thurs.	Fri.	Sat.	Sun.	Holiday
922	MU	L	101	1231	1	1	1	1	1	1	1	1
923	TR	L	101	430	1	1	1	1	1	1	1	
923	TR	L	501	630	1	1	1	1	1			
923	TR	L	901	1031	1	1	1	1	1			
923	TR	L	1101	1231	1	1	1	1	1	1	1	
923	TR	M	501	630						1	1	
923	TR	M	701	831	1	1	1	1	1	1	1	
923	TR	M	901	1031						1	1	
923	TR	M	101	1231								1
924	TR	L	101	430	1	1	1	1	1	1	1	
924	TR	L	501	630	1	1	1	1	1			
924	TR	L	901	1031	1	1	1	1	1			
924	TR	L	1101	1231	1	1	1	1	1	1	1	
924	TR	M	501	630						1	1	
924	TR	M	701	831	1	1	1	1	1	1	1	
924	TR	M	901	1031						1	1	
924	TR	M	101	1231								1
925	TR	L	101	430	1	1	1	1	1	1	1	
925	TR	L	501	630	1	1	1	1	1			
925	TR	L	901	1031	1	1	1	1	1			
925	TR	L	1101	1231	1	1	1	1	1	1	1	
925	TR	M	501	630						1	1	
925	TR	M	701	831	1	1	1	1	1	1	1	
925	TR	M	901	1031						1	1	
925	TR	M	101	1231								1
926	TR	L	101	1231	1	1	1	1	1	1	1	1
927	TR	L	101	1231	1	1	1	1	1	1	1	1
928	TR	L	101	1231	1	1	1	1	1	1	1	1
929	TR	L	101	1231	1	1	1	1	1	1	1	1
930	TR	L	101	1231	1	1	1	1	1	1	1	1
931	TR	L	101	1231	1	1	1	1	1	1	1	1
932	TR	L	101	1231	1	1	1	1	1	1	1	1
933	TR	L	101	430	1	1	1	1	1	1	1	
933	TR	L	501	630	1	1	1	1	1			
933	TR	L	901	1031	1	1	1	1	1			
933	TR	L	1101	1231	1	1	1	1	1	1	1	
933	TR	M	501	630						1	1	
933	TR	M	701	831	1	1	1	1	1	1	1	
933	TR	M	901	1031						1	1	
933	TR	M	101	1231								1
934	TR	L	101	1231	1	1	1	1	1	1	1	1
935	TR	L	101	1231	1	1	1	1	1	1	1	1
937	P	L	101	331	1	1	1	1	1	1	1	
937	P	L	401	1031	1	1	1	1	1			
937	P	L	1101	1231	1	1	1	1	1	1	1	
937	P	M	401	1031						1	1	
937	P	M	101	1231								1
938	P	L	101	331	1	1	1	1	1	1	1	
938	P	L	401	1031	1	1	1	1	1			

continued

The pilot survey prework spreadsheet consists of all the sites classified into site-types and use-levels for the entire 2007 calendar year. The pilot survey actually used only those site days from June 1 through August 14, 2007. The site names that correspond to the site numbers can be found in table 1 (continued)

Site number	Site-type	Use-level	Begin	End	Mon.	Tues.	Wed.	Thurs.	Fri.	Sat.	Sun.	Holiday
938	P	L	1101	1231	1	1	1	1	1	1	1	
938	P	M	401	1031						1	1	
938	P	M	101	1231								1
942	TR	L	101	430	1	1	1	1	1	1	1	
942	TR	L	501	630	1	1	1	1	1			
942	TR	L	901	1031	1	1	1	1	1			
942	TR	L	1101	1231	1	1	1	1	1	1	1	
942	TR	M	501	630						1	1	
942	TR	M	701	831	1	1	1	1	1	1	1	
942	TR	M	901	1031						1	1	
942	TR	M	101	1231								1
946	TR	L	101	1231	1	1	1	1	1	1	1	1
948	TR	L	101	1231	1	1	1	1	1	1	1	1
949	P	L	101	331	1	1	1	1	1	1	1	
949	P	L	401	630	1	1	1	1	1			
949	P	L	901	1031	1	1	1	1	1			
949	P	L	1101	1231	1	1	1	1	1	1	1	
949	P	M	401	630						1	1	
949	P	M	701	831	1	1	1	1	1	1	1	
949	P	M	901	1031						1	1	
949	P	M	101	1231								1
950	P	L	101	331	1	1	1	1	1	1	1	
950	P	L	401	630	1	1	1	1	1			
950	P	L	901	1031	1	1	1	1	1			
950	P	L	1101	1231	1	1	1	1	1	1	1	
950	P	M	401	630						1	1	
950	P	M	701	831	1	1	1	1	1	1	1	
950	P	M	901	1031						1	1	
950	P	M	101	1231								1
951	P	L	101	1231	1	1	1	1	1	1	1	1
953	MU	L	101	430	1	1	1	1	1	1	1	1
953	MU	L	801	1231	1	1	1	1	1	1	1	1
953	MU	M	501	731	1	1	1	1	1	1	1	1
954	MU	L	101	331	1	1	1	1	1	1	1	
954	MU	L	401	630	1	1	1	1	1			
954	MU	L	901	1031	1	1	1	1	1			
954	MU	L	1101	1231	1	1	1	1	1	1	1	
954	MU	M	401	630						1	1	
954	MU	M	701	831	1	1	1	1	1	1	1	
954	MU	M	901	1031						1	1	
954	MU	M	101	1231								1
955	MU	L	101	331	1	1	1	1	1	1	1	
955	MU	L	401	531	1	1	1	1	1			
955	MU	L	901	1130	1	1	1	1	1			
955	MU	L	1201	1231	1	1	1	1	1	1	1	
955	MU	M	401	531						1	1	
955	MU	M	601	831	1	1	1	1	1			
955	MU	M	1001	1130						1	1	
955	MU	H	601	930						1	1	

continued

Appendix B

The pilot survey prework spreadsheet consists of all the sites classified into site-types and use-levels for the entire 2007 calendar year. The pilot survey actually used only those site days from June 1 through August 14, 2007. The site names that correspond to the site numbers can be found in table 1 (continued)

Site number	Site-type	Use-level	Begin	End	Mon.	Tues.	Wed.	Thurs.	Fri.	Sat.	Sun.	Holiday
955	MU	H	101	1231								1
957	MU	L	101	331	1	1	1	1	1	1	1	
957	MU	L	401	630	1	1	1	1	1			
957	MU	L	901	1031	1	1	1	1	1			
957	MU	L	1101	1231	1	1	1	1	1	1	1	
957	MU	M	401	630						1	1	
957	MU	M	701	831	1	1	1	1	1	1	1	
957	MU	M	901	1031						1	1	
957	MU	M	101	1231								1
958	TR	L	101	430	1	1	1	1	1	1	1	
958	TR	L	501	630	1	1	1	1	1			
958	TR	L	901	1031	1	1	1	1	1			
958	TR	L	1101	1231	1	1	1	1	1	1	1	
958	TR	M	501	630						1	1	
958	TR	M	701	831	1	1	1	1	1	1	1	
958	TR	M	901	1031						1	1	
958	TR	M	101	1231								1
959	TR	L	101	1231	1	1	1	1	1	1	1	1
961	TR	L	101	1231	1	1	1	1	1	1	1	1
962	TR	L	101	1231	1	1	1	1	1	1	1	1
963	TR	L	101	630	1	1	1	1	1	1	1	
963	TR	L	901	1231	1	1	1	1	1	1	1	
963	TR	M	701	831	1	1	1	1	1	1	1	
963	TR	M	101	1231								1
965	P	L	101	1231	1	1	1	1	1	1	1	1
967	P	L	101	1231	1	1	1	1	1	1	1	1
970	P	L	101	1231	1	1	1	1	1	1	1	1
973	TR	L	101	1231	1	1	1	1	1	1	1	1
975	P	L	101	1231	1	1	1	1	1	1	1	1
981	TR	L	101	1231	1	1	1	1	1	1	1	1
982	TR	L	101	1231	1	1	1	1	1	1	1	1
984	P	L	101	1231	1	1	1	1	1	1	1	1
987	TR	L	101	630	1	1	1	1	1	1	1	1
987	TR	L	901	1231	1	1	1	1	1	1	1	1
987	TR	M	701	831	1	1	1	1	1	1	1	1
988	TR	L	101	430	1	1	1	1	1	1	1	
988	TR	L	501	1031	1	1	1	1	1			
988	TR	L	1101	1231	1	1	1	1	1	1	1	
988	TR	M	501	1031						1	1	
988	TR	M	101	1231								1
993	TR	L	101	1231	1	1	1	1	1	1	1	1
994	P	L	101	1231	1	1	1	1	1	1	1	1
995	P	L	101	1231	1	1	1	1	1	1	1	1
998	MU	L	101	1231	1	1	1	1	1	1	1	1
999	MU	L	101	331	1	1	1	1	1	1	1	
999	MU	L	401	531	1	1	1	1	1			
999	MU	L	901	1130	1	1	1	1	1			
999	MU	L	1201	1231	1	1	1	1	1	1	1	
999	MU	M	401	531						1	1	

continued

The pilot survey prework spreadsheet consists of all the sites classified into site-types and use-levels for the entire 2007 calendar year. The pilot survey actually used only those site days from June 1 through August 14, 2007. The site names that correspond to the site numbers can be found in table 1 (continued)

Site number	Site-type	Use-level	Begin	End	Mon.	Tues.	Wed.	Thurs.	Fri.	Sat.	Sun.	Holiday
999	MU	M	601	831	1	1	1	1	1			
999	MU	M	1101	1130						1	1	
999	MU	H	601	1031						1	1	
999	MU	H	101	1231								1
1000	MU	L	101	331	1	1	1	1	1	1	1	
1000	MU	L	1101	1130	1	1	1	1	1			
1000	MU	L	1201	1231	1	1	1	1	1	1	1	
1000	MU	M	401	531	1	1	1	1	1	1	1	
1000	MU	M	601	1031	1	1	1	1	1			
1000	MU	M	1101	1130						1	1	
1000	MU	H	601	1031						1	1	
1000	MU	H	101	1231								1
1001	MU	L	101	1231	1	1	1	1	1	1	1	1
1002	MU	L	101	1231	1	1	1	1	1	1	1	1
1003	TR	L	101	1231	1	1	1	1	1	1	1	1
1004	TR	L	101	1231	1	1	1	1	1	1	1	1
1005	P	L	101	1231	1	1	1	1	1	1	1	1
1007	P	L	101	1231	1	1	1	1	1	1	1	1
1009	TR	L	101	1231	1	1	1	1	1	1	1	1
1010	TR	L	101	1231	1	1	1	1	1	1	1	1
1011	TR	L	101	1231	1	1	1	1	1	1	1	1
1015	TR	L	101	531	1	1	1	1	1	1	1	
1015	TR	L	801	1231	1	1	1	1	1	1	1	
1015	TR	L	101	1231								1
1015	TR	M	601	731	1	1	1	1	1	1	1	
1016	P	L	101	1231	1	1	1	1	1	1	1	1
1019	TR	L	101	1231	1	1	1	1	1	1	1	1

Note: ATCH = Appalachian Trail Conservancy Headquarters; TR = trail/road; HF = Harpers Ferry; P = parking; MU = multiple use; L= low; M = medium; H = high..